DENNIS
POTTER

fr. Dennis Potter at Oxford, the editor of *Isis*, 1958

DENNIS
POTTER

Peter Stead

Border Lines Series Editor
John Powell Ward

SEREN BOOKS

For Elizabeth

SEREN BOOKS is the book imprint of
Poetry Wales Press Ltd
Andmar House, Tondu Road, Bridgend, Mid Glamorgan

The text © Peter Stead, 1993
Editorial, Afterword © John Powell Ward, 1993

A British Library cataloguing in publication data record
is available from the CIP office

ISBN 1-85411-071-3
1-85411-072-1 paperback

Cover photograph by Jane Bown

*Seren Books works with the financial assistance of the
Welsh Arts Council*

Printed in Palatino by
The Alden Press, Oxford

Contents

List of Illustrations

Acknowledgements

I have been fascinated by the work of Dennis Potter since I first watched the Nigel Barton plays in 1965. What I offer here is a straightforward critical assessment of his major works based entirely on my own personal reactions. As a historian I have also attempted to place him as a writer into a very specific English context. My thanks, of course, above all go to him.

I met Dennis Potter only after the book was written. On a memorable afternoon at the Hay-on-Wye Festival of Literature I interviewed the playwright in a hot marquee in front of over four hundred enthralled ticket-holders. After ninety minutes both participants were exhausted but we had conspired to provide first-class entertainment — perhaps the best England-Wales contest for several seasons.

My thanks go to all the production companies and individuals who have contributed to the making of Dennis Potter's plays and films and to the BFI for arranging for me to view so many of them. I received magnificent encouragement and much practical assistance from my editor, John Powell Ward, and as always my wife Elizabeth joined with me in what was really another team effort.

Peter Stead
July 1993

Photographic Acknowledgements

The publisher gratefully acknowledges the assistance of Hulton Deutsch (frontispiece), the BFI (3, 8, 16), the BBC (1, 2, 4, 5, 6, 7, 9, 10, 11, 12, 13, 14, 15), Stephen Morley (16), London Weekend Television (3).

The Drama of the A40

In his 1978 television play *Pennies From Heaven* Dennis Potter quite beautifully paces a blend of incident and premonition that inexorably leads the salesman Arthur Parker towards his death by hanging. The touches of irony are really more like teasing drumbeats as they blatantly herald the inevitable dramatic coda. In the sixth and final episode, *Says My Heart*, we sense the end as Arthur and his mistress Eileen decide that they can no longer remain in hiding at the farm; now they both want to return to London where she can at least earn money as a prostitute whilst Arthur stays indoors listening to records and going out only to see movies. In their car they head south. Soon they come to the main road and at the junction we, the viewers, see them from above and behind as they approach and halt at a huge signpost, the two arms of which have all the appearance and heavy significance of a cross. By turning right Arthur and Eileen could once again travel west along the A40, passing the field where the police believe Arthur to have committed a brutal sex murder and then the city where they had first met, so as to arrive at the Forest of Dean village where their passionate affair had begun. It is not the road to Gloucester, however, that the couple now choose but rather that which heads east to London. Within minutes Arthur is in custody and we know that tragedy is imminent. For a moment that Gloucester-London signpost neatly reminds us of the whole axis on which the fate of Arthur and Eileen and the whole action of *Pennies From Heaven* has been based. It is not inappropriate that *Pennies From Heaven*, the mini-series that confirmed Dennis Potter's international reputation as a brilliantly successful and innovative television dramatist, should have been essentially a drama of the old A40 road. The eight-hour play tackles huge themes as it sets out to encapsulate the many strands that made up the English experience in the Great Depression of the 1930s. We are invited to compare and contrast suburban, urban and rural values and to contemplate the contribution of commerce, religion, sex and popular culture in determining individual freedom and fulfilment at a time when many economic and social obstacles seemed to constrain the aspirations of ordinary folk. Potter's simple plot effortlessly incorporates all these themes and to a considerable extent it is precisely the organising notion of the A40 road which allows him to achieve that end. In *Pennies From Heaven*, as in so much of Potter's work, whether it be television drama, fiction or essays, ideas and action are worked out on the basis of an interaction between Gloucestershire's Forest of Dean and London.

Teasingly Potter has suggested that there is an element of laziness in his continuing dependence on the A40 axis, for indeed it is always easier for an author to set his fictional action in and to select his non-fictional examples from the world he knows best. 'That is why', one of his fictional voices reflects, 'we get so few English novels located in places like a Tibetan monastery, a Peruvian tin mine or the Ford Motor Works at Dagenham'. Certainly Potter has chosen to write extensively about the world he knew best. In 1960 he confessed to having 'a close knowledge of only two areas: Fulham and the Forest of Dean'. Now thirty years later, apart from an acquaintance with Hollywood, little has changed and Potter continues to live in and imaginatively to explore the two communities that were the world of his parents and his own childhood.

The continuing interaction between the Forest and London is quite a remarkable feature of his own history. He was born in the Forest in 1935, the son of a coalminer. His mother, however, was a Londoner and when he was fourteen she took her family to live in the city where she had grown up. His parents were to return to Gloucestershire but Potter stayed on with his relatives in Hammersmith and continued his education at St Clement Danes Grammar School. After National Service and three years at Oxford he returned to London and began a career as a journalist first with the BBC and then in Fleet Street. He stood as the Labour candidate for East Hertfordshire in the 1964 General Election and, following that defeat and the further development of an illness that has been diagnosed as psoriatic arthropathy, he and his wife Margaret decided to return to their native West of England. They bought a house in Ross-on-Wye and have lived there ever since. It has been very much a family home with the three children living either at home or nearby, and it was here that Potter was to sustain his remarkable literary output. All the while, of course, there have been trips to London to deal with agents and producers, to supervise and more recently to direct productions, to broadcast and to meet with journalists. He is still travelling that same axis taken originally by his mother and then later by Arthur and Eileen in *Pennies From Heaven* although his fiction suggests that it is the railway line to Paddington that has now replaced the old A40 as the trigger to his imagination. What is perhaps most remarkable in this story of loyalty to what we may term "a family line" is that Potter's home in Ross, that charming medieval but now largely Victorian town that stands on a red sandstone promontory above the River Wye affording views of the adjacent Welsh mountains, is only eight miles from the coalmining community of Berry Hill where he grew up. That eight miles contains some of the most spectacular scenery in southern England, not least the deep gorge on the Wye at Symonds Yat. Coalminer's son he may have been but Dennis Potter was raised and has once again chosen to live in an area that seems to exemplify the sheer loveliness of England. Not surprisingly, as an author he has often chosen to examine those forces and influences that have threatened that loveliness.

The London-Forest of Dean nexus cries out for analysis and certainly that will be one of the central themes of this study. There are many dangers, though, in opting for any autobiographical interpretation of Potter's dramatic and fictional output. Critics and academics cannot say that they have not been warned. Over and over again the author has frightened commentators off. He has pointedly explained that he is a writer of fictions, someone who has struggled to overcome 'second-order memories (nostalgia), received opinions (prejudices), dismay or resentment' in order to find his own literary voice. He has chosen to become a dramatist and therefore not an autobiographer nor, initially, a writer of novels (a 'fraudulent' form, as one of his characters suggests, for 'they pretend to tell you too much'). Very simply,

11

then, his message is 'that a play is a play is a play' and I for one am totally happy to accept that instruction. Potter has an *alter ego* spell out the point that 'only a fool or charlatan will maintain that an author and his leading character are genetically or spiritually conjoined by things darker and stronger than the sweet grace of pure creative imagination'. Point taken.

I set out, then, to pay full tribute to a remarkably inventive creative imagination anticipating the satisfaction there will be in experiencing once again the thrills, the shocks, the challenge and the sheer entertainment afforded by his television plays. I will, however, also be writing about Dennis Potter the man and making every effort to assess his place in recent British history not only as a television writer but also as a cultural critic and cultural force. For all his protestations that the play is the thing there are many aspects of his career which invite cultural analysis. He tends now to play down the significance of his first two published works, dismissing them as 'cant' and a 'shuffling through cards marked "class" or "England" or "alienation"', but *The Glittering Coffin* (1960) and *The Changing Forest* (1962) were important reflections of the kind of intellectual and social anger that was changing Britain and especially the basis of its educational, journalistic and artistic thinking in the late fifties and early sixties. Furthermore, they remain an invaluable introduction to nearly all Potter's drama and fiction. Clearly what was to be his unique literary voice began to develop as he began to investigate the individual consequences of what he had assumed in these early works to be more general social forces. To a quite remarkable extent nearly all his stories have been set within a society whose conflicting sub-cultural and class values were first identified and evaluated in these early essays. Within a few years Potter had dramatized these same observations and judgements in the two *Nigel Barton* plays (1965). One is not necessarily being foolish or cretinous in advancing the argument that Nigel Barton is not only a useful key to the Britain of his day but also an important clue in any understanding of his creator. There was a lot of Barton in the Potter of 1965; there is a lot of him in the Potter of today.

As is the case with other authors one can easily detect the way in which Potter has been sickened and angered by interviewers asking about or critics just assuming the autobiographical element in his work. His response has been the deflection of his anger into what he admits is a certain 'facetiousness'. He has embarked on an elaborate game which has developed really into part of the very package in which his work comes to us, his audience. The play is the thing, we are told, and so the author should not matter or even be seen. He might not often be seen but certainly the voice is heard, either in the written form in countless press interviews or increasingly in radio interviews in which his highly distinctive voice, with what one American critic described as its 'squelched vowels', its rural burr, its careful precision and its invitation to intimacy, can be immediately recognised. Essentially Potter uses the interviews both to publicise and to set the scene for his plays. Perhaps he is hoping to head off further journalistic speculation about what is bound to be taken as yet another chapter of autobiography. Certainly he is teasing his audiences, for protestations about the autonomy of the play will always come alongside indications of his own despair and torment as well as tantalising biographical snippets. He could reasonably claim that those seeking the definitive story of his life should just read all the interviews.

He is playing a game but he does this to some effect. He is establishing his presence and existence as the author so that audiences should know something about the process of creation. His contempt for those who think that he has been dramatizing his own experiences is equalled by his concern that audiences should know how memory is only one element in the complicated and painful process of giving artistic expression to the welter of one's own emotions. As he reflects on whether the childhood recalled was one he had actually experienced or whether 'we all live in a sort of exile from the lost land of our childhood' so he reveals both the ache and the need that ties him to familiar material and yet also that vast sense of distance and alienation that artistic endeavour has to negotiate. The voice we read and listen to is always reminding us that it is the Dennis Potter of today we should be interested in and the edge that the best of those interviews have is there because nobody is more aware than the author himself that he is only as interesting and relevant as his latest play. I love to hear him speak. In the Britain of today both his accent and his tone are unique. He invites serious reflection and it is important that we listen. Of few other people can it be said that the voice is the key to the man. He wants us to pay attention and to understand. That voice is as important in establishing his identity as his apparently more accessible but perhaps more complex plays.

Fully to appreciate Potter one should play his game with him. The best introduction remains his first novel, very appropriately entitled *Hide and Seek*, which was published in 1973. The tease starts on page one as we learn that the tale's protagonist has one of those characteristically and quintessentially English surnames that denote traditional rural crafts: in this case not a potter, as it happens, but a miller. We are introduced then to Daniel Miller whose life is a mess and whose chief problem is his feeling that he is nothing but a character in a book and that his every action and thought was controlled by The Author. On page thirty-eight (after 13,000 words) and in the words of the book's cover blurb 'we learn that he is right'. Miller is merely a character in a tale and now The Author steps forward to identify (though not to name) himself. Thereafter Dennis Potter plays a marvellous game of analysing the nature of the novel in general as he contemplates the nature of sexual desire, of illness, of psychology, of religion and of literary criticism through the voice of either Daniel Miller or The Author. Both voices too ask us to consider the various influences of West London and the Forest of Dean. Inevitably *Hide and Seek* is an infuriating book but it is also extremely entertaining and it is absolutely essential to any understanding of the way in which Potter, when he has subsequently come out of hiding, wants to be seen as The Author, a character or rather an agent in our culture who exists alongside his works and comments on them. As always Potter is urging us to concentrate our attention on The Author, not necessarily the one who appears in *Hide and Seek* (who is of course a fictional character), rather than to go in search of a Dennis Potter 'hiding behind the skirts of invented characters'.

Certainly one of the fascinations of examining Potter's career and works is this dimension of him as an Author within the Culture, as someone whose creative process is triggered off by his wanting to debate his own passionate concerns whether they be social, political, religious or artistic in the context of specific class and commercial pressures. This dimension is far more evident and important in his case than it is in the careers of other writers who have been taken as being either more representative or more significant in post-1945 Britain. In this respect it is interesting to compare Potter with those contemporary American writers who have been aware of their roles as Authors. Norman Mailer's analysis of the anti-Vietnam demonstration in Washington in 1967 was enriched enormously by his writing about himself in the third person and by his fundamental realisation that the Mailer who demonstrated and was arrested was both The Novelist and The Historian. Potter and Mailer are very different writers but we insular British can deepen our understanding of the former by considering the American writer's considerable sense of himself, vanity if you like, his sheer pride in the power that good writing has to explain (both to The Author himself and to the readers), his continuing need to promote himself as a commentator on his own work and his total lack of fear in experimenting so as to keep his work before as large an audience as possible.

The other useful comparison is with Philip Roth, an author who has always been at his most effective when writing about a Jewish family in New Jersey and in particular about the relationship between the parents and their college-educated son who has become a successful and popular novelist by writing about his own childhood and early career. The most memorable moments in Roth are always those when his character Zuckerman smashes taboos and writes directly about personal and family experiences. 'Well Nathan', says Zuckerman's father in *The Ghost Writer*, 'you certainly didn't leave anything out, did you?' It is quite impossible to read this without being a little embarrassed and, of course, without wondering if Mr Roth Senior ever said those precise words to a young Philip. Is Zuckerman Roth? Well, to explain things to his readers The Novelist, having written his fiction, then turned to autobiography. Having written a novel entitled *The Ghost Writer* he then provides an autobiography simply called *The Facts* in which Philip Roth writes to Zuckerman and receives a reply. All this is in order to explain 'that there is a significant gap between the autobiographical writer that I am thought to be and the autobiographical writer that I am'. Again Potter and Roth are worlds apart; inevitably very different novels have come out of the miner's cottage in Gloucestershire and the insurance-salesman's suburban home in Newark. Certainly language plays very different roles in the one culture that leaves so much unsaid as compared to the other which almost compulsively articulates emotions and fears. Nevertheless Zuckerman Senior's 'Well Nathan' reminds one of nothing so much as how Dennis Potter has his characters Nigel Barton and his father react to Nigel's television interview. 'They cut it, Dad', explains the son; 'you cut me lad', answers the coalmining father. Potter and Roth have travelled the same road. A writer has to distance himself from his memories even as he feeds off them and in that distancing he becomes an Author and that Author has a complex relationship not only with the writer when young but even with the writer of today. Both Potter and Roth are to be admired for their courage and for the fascinating insight they have given us into what writing really means. It has been said of Anthony Powell that his autobiographical volumes are dull because all his talent had gone into writing the twelve volumes of *A Dance to the Music of Time*: the novel was his true autobiography. Powell, one suspected, was a dull man who had written a great book. Other writers are as interesting as their works but largely, of course, because they are consciously writers tantalised by the notion of using words and characters to say something complex and new.

They have embarked on a venture which is often as frightening as it is rewarding and we the benefactors should at least try to understand. It is in this context that I look at Dennis Potter.

Does Class Matter?

'Does class matter?' It was the asking of that question which launched Dennis Potter's career. It was the title of the 1958 BBC programme in which the young Oxford student came before the cameras to talk as openly and controversially about the prison-like system of class much as he had done earlier in the pages of *The New Statesman*. Such boldness and honesty were a godsend for the popular press. The headline in *Reynolds News* was 'Miner's son at Oxford Ashamed of Home' whilst *The Daily Herald* highlighted the dilemma of a student who 'could no longer talk to his father' but who admitted to being thrilled when 'his college servant called him "Sir"'. Rarely can an ambitious young writer have been given his subject and his modus operandi in such a dramatic way. A personal response to class and the differing values of the West and the South of England, especially as mediated by the BBC and Fleet Street, was what was called for. Potter's response was his first book (written as an undergraduate) and then the writing and presenting of his own television film which became the basis of his second book. After a short interval those same themes were the core inspiration for the two Nigel Barton films which were, of course, the works which gave him his first experience of both artistic success and notoriety. Over the years Potter has somewhat changed his emphasis, not least in going for greater psychological depth, but a very strong case can be made for the view that in many respects he is still thinking about that simple question about class which his interviewer Christopher Mayhew had put to him in 1958.

That particular question had been asked in 1958 as part of the process whereby television was beginning to reflect the changing social composition of those who shaped cultural life in Britain. It was obvious that a new generation of academics and authors were fully prepared to talk honestly about how life-styles had changed in their own relatively short careers. What precisely happened to Britain's "chattering classes" at the time of the Suez crisis has been much debated and certainly far too much emphasis has been placed on the literary output of middle-class writers like Amis, Larkin and Osborne who had no real reason to be angry. What was really significant about these five or so years after Suez was the way in which working-class writers suddenly had the confidence to write about their own backgrounds as they sensed the relevance of class and regional differences to any prospect of cultural and political change in Great Britain. Cultural transformations of this dimension occur only as a result of a complex interplay of forces and historians have rightly stressed the role of grammar schools and the scholarship system, the impact of National Service, prosperity and the theatrical style of the Macmillan government. Two other influences are perhaps in need of more emphasis. The changing nature of both television and the press was, as Arthur Marwick has indicated, vital in making cultural innovation newsworthy and so reports of revolutionary and shocking happenings tended to become self-fulfilling prophecies. John Osborne needed his Kenneth Tynan. As Tynan convinced his thousands of readers that great things were happening in tiny London theatres so the whole nature of the Sunday press began to change as did its relationship with its readers. It was prophetic indeed that audiences' first glimpse of Osborne's Jimmy Porter had been of him reading the Sunday papers. The other great influence was the impact of the United States. For a generation there had been much British interest in aspects of American popular culture but it was only really in the 1950s, with the coming of a new prosperity, that British intellectuals realised that mass consumption and mass culture opened up new horrors and new possibilties. Attitudes to what Jimmy Porter identified as 'the American age' were riddled with contradictions. Materialism and mediocrity beckoned and yet continually from North America there came startling cultural innovation which somehow seemed related to more democratic values.

The whole culture seemed suddenly to be inviting comment on

how the caution of what was to be termed the British Establishment could be replaced by more democratic energies. The really essential changes came within the sphere of education and it was academics who really provided the vital influences and texts. Quite suddenly at universities the nature of English and history as subjects changed and out of the blue there appeared the social sciences. It was the appearance of Richard Hoggart's *The Uses of Literacy* and Raymond Williams' *Culture and Society* in 1958 which really confirmed that a new chapter had opened in the cultural life of the nation. Suddenly everything that the working-class novelists and playwrights and the new social and economic historians were trying to do fell into place and all the while undergraduates who had felt the full excitement of these new texts were heading off into the new jobs that were opening up in television and Fleet Street. The interplay of influences was undoubtedly complex, but the term "Hoggart-Williams revolution" seems far more appropriate than that of "angry young men", for it was that crucial conveyor belt of ideas and personnel that ran between universities and the media that allowed creative artists to feel that their backgrounds were relevant and that somehow the future was to be theirs. In almost every respect Dennis Potter was part of the very process that both created and sustained the Hoggart-Williams revolution.

So much was happening in the Britain of the 1950s that it is hardly surprising that talented young people whose own lives had been transformed by educational and career opportunities should develop feelings that the country could be reshaped in their own image if only the remaining barrier could be overcome. Potter the student knew that it was arrogant of him to write such a book as *The Glittering Coffin* but he was fully aware that the time was ripe for such a protest and that people of his kind were being encouraged to get on platforms or to move centre stage. All over the land, and not least in the places where it really mattered — Oxford, Cambridge and London — , there were audiences, readers, senior common room members and editors who were inviting young people to see what they could get away with in terms of literary or academic anger. 'Tell us about your background', they were saying, 'prove your class credentials'; 'tell us how bad things are', 'but do it brilliantly', 'do it with style' and above all 'write it well'.

At New College, Oxford, Potter was responding to a trend, to a fashion and to a challenge that could only do him good. He had been an outstanding student: he was openly to boast about his having edited both *Isis* and the Labour Club's *Clarion* and he had been prominent in dramatic, political and Union activities. His talent had been spotted by London editors and producers and in quite a direct sense *The Glittering Coffin* was written both to guarantee his immediate translation to an influential position in the national media and to provide a prospectus for what he assumed he would be allowed to achieve as a columnist, as a broadcaster or, more likely, as a politician.

His first book was written, then, not in any bare garret or by candlelight between shifts at t' mill. It was written fairly near the centre of things and its concerns and style were very much sanctioned and even commissioned by forces of growth and change within the culture. The author could apologise at the time for its 'arrogance' and 'highly impressionistic' nature but he was really doing no more than was expected of him. In several respects this first book reads like a summary of the anger and protest England had experienced since John Osborne had launched a new era in 1956. Jimmy Porter could very easily have written sections of the book. Certainly there are whole passages that seemed inspired by Richard Hoggart, not least that on women's magazines. The essays in Tom Maschler's collection *Declarations* were dismissed as 'the yelp' of irritated intellectuals but one assumes that Potter's own copy of that basic text-book of "anger" was well-thumbed. Later Potter was openly to admit that much of his first two books had consisted of 'shuffling through cards marked "class" or "England" or "alienation"' and that the appearance of weighty original thought had been illusory. Certainly *The Glittering Coffin* was essentially journalism and was meant very specifically to convey what was not just a personal protest but rather what intelligent people who really cared were thinking about the state of the nation. What Potter had done was to fit his own experience and to prove his own class credentials within what had become an accepted format. What his later reservations and dissociation ignore, however, is the extent to which even in his first book he had found a truly distinctive voice and method and had even betrayed feelings that he has never to this day abandoned.

The Glittering Coffin is as much a monologue as it is a mono-graph. It is a later familiarity with the broadcast voice of Potter that informs that judgement but one suspects that even readers new to this author will detect the immediacy and directness of tone. There is a confessional and careful reflectiveness here that was always to be this writer's hallmark. Osborne too had been lucky in the way that he had directly found a voice that invited attention, but from the outset the former actor in him had opted for rhetoric. Potter by contrast seems to have been a natural radio broadcaster, a consequence no doubt of many hours of listening, for here in spite of the occasional flashy phrase what one detects is a controlled conversational pace in which general analysis and observation are always firmly linked to personal experience and most often a real sense of personal regret. Somehow society, the culture, the nation have failed, not least because they have let him down. We are being asked to consider vastly broad and interna-tional forces of social change, we are never allowed to forget that this is a vital moment in the history of the nation, and yet for all the attempts to provide rational academic analysis, to find the historian's tone, the touchstone is always that of the emotions. The vital experience has been personal and until this moment private. The key passage in this first book is that in which the author maintains that 'talking about class in highly personal terms is a shocking and embarrassing thing for an Englishman to do'. 'Shocking', yes, that was very much part of what the second half of the fifties was about: suddenly the nation was asked to confront working-class accents, working-class phenomena such as ex-cessive drinking and unwanted pregnancies and working-class habitats such as the eponymous kitchen sink. But 'embarrassing'? That is a slightly different note. Certainly by 1960 readers and audiences would be aware of how heroes and heroines from humble backgrounds could easily be shown up and caught off guard in the world of the middle-class; there are elements of that in Wesker, Alun Owen and Hoggart. But in general in the lit-erature and drama of the period it is working-class arrogance and *braggadocio* that carry the day. The predominant images of those years are of Alan Sillitoe's Arthur Seaton as brought to life by Albert Finney and of John Braine's Joe Lampton courtesy of Laurence Harvey; the predominant voice is possibly that of Harold Pinter's scathing, carping, brutal low-life characters. If embarrassment there was, then the writers ensured that it was most keenly felt by middle-class hosts or audiences.

This passage in Potter is completed by two further sentences. In the first he states that 'there is a kind of pornography about the subject [of class], an atmosphere of whispered asides and lowered eyes'. Now we have certainly entered "Potterland" and the next sentence confirms it: 'It is too much like small boys discussing sex in the school playground'. Sex is the most private of all concerns, the most darkly hidden and deeply personal aspect of our own identity, the part of ourself most firmly kept in check by social taboo, convention and linguistic inhibition and inadequacy. And yet Potter now reveals that for him personal details of class come into the same category. All the time we are invited to reflect on how that immediate television and Fleet Street fame had caught him on the raw; class, family, confession and fame had come to him in one package; he was stung, he was embarrassed but all the same he was given a career and a literary seam to work.

What was to be Potter's personal world is there, then, in *The Glittering Coffin* and these are themes to which we must later return. The passage quoted is undoubtedly the most interesting, tantalising and presageful in the book but we should also note other hints of what was to come. When arguing that class did indeed matter more in 1960 than in 1945 Potter again sought to explain its sheer power and unrelenting quality by claiming that 'class pulses outward in a distinctly physical beat, a constant rhythm of hundreds of minor habits and characteristics'. Clearly this is a subject he will not easily abandon. Two years later in *The Changing Forest* he was to refer to 'the stale, sickly smell of class and condescension which seems inseparable from the condition of England'. Such feelings, it would seem, could hardly be assuaged by mere political protest and social reform. When analysing the national trend towards conformity he suggests that the TUC was 'a kind of collective Judas'. This is a strikingly bitter phrase in a work of cultural analysis and one that again injects a personal note, a Nonconformist voice, something not often heard in the very largely secular protests of the "angry young man". As Potter first introduces us to his childhood experience of two different worlds, the Forest and the City, so he tells of how at the age of ten and on his first visit to London 'I cried all through a hot, noisy night, cried with the kind of sick passion of those who love a place almost as much as they love a person'. One knows instinctively that this is not affectation just as one suspects that those ten-year old tears were not the last. 'Love' and 'sick passion' are again notes that take us away from the macho world of fifties anger. To write about class and personal experience is to generate 'misunderstanding' and 'stress'. The dilemmas are real, for 'when do love and respect shade into a kind of benevolent condescension?' For all the sociological sweep it is very much a personal honesty that we are asked to consider. And yet the plaintive tone of the autobiographical snippets can still be given a mischievous, teasing and cryptic quality that shows that the author is very much enjoying himself. There is after all fun for him in writing. The sentence (written, remember, by the undergraduate Potter) 'Entering the lounge bar sends up the price of a drink, and that's not all it does' seems to me to herald the mature writer as does nothing else in this his first book. Imagine it said in the Potter accent and you are on the way to understanding his work.

The Glittering Coffin was written by a young man who was very conscious that he was a part of a new generation, one of those who was 'on the move' out of working-class homes and districts and into colleges and careers that would allow influence and possibly bring about change. He was also well aware that his experience of being 'on the move' was one of the most dramatic that could be conceived and that, of course, his reflections were thought of as ideal television. All over the country the sons and daughters of respectable artisan families were now making their ways from their terraced homes or from council semis to colleges of one sort or another, and many would take with them the familiar accents and cultural values of the country's large urban agglomerations. Potter's case though was altogether of a different order. Quite justifiably he thought of himself as having been translated from one extreme to another. He knew what the essential truth had been and so there was no deception in the way the young "writer" sought to drive home the drama of his experience by heightening the contrast. For the moment he leaves aside the fact of his two years National Service as a War Office clerk, an experience, of course, that made him and his kind into very special undergraduates, and there is also no mention of his years of secondary education in London. Rather we are invited to consider the story of a young man who had gone straight from the Forest of Dean to one of the country's most glittering and ancient educational establishments, New College, Oxford, a transformation that Potter further heightens by telling of how his last night had been spent with his parents having a 'farewell drink' at the Berry Hill Workingmen's Club. The prentice author then is taking his stand. This was his base, this was where his identity had been defined. Here at the bar the locals come up to wish him well. 'Thou go all the road, butty', says one, 'only don't forget where tha come from, oot?'

Where indeed did Dennis Potter come from and has he ever forgotten it? The story goes that at Oxford many of his fellow students just assumed that the Forest of Dean was in the North of England; that was where bright working-class boys were supposed to come from. In fact Potter had travelled only sixty miles, had in fact just crossed the Cotswold range. He had come to the centre of things from one of the most neglected and distinctive pockets of England. It is not difficult to make a case for the singularity of the Forest: it is, as Humphrey Phelps has maintained, 'a country on its own'. In essence it is a triangular forested plateau (Potter has referred to it as being 'heart- shaped') clearly bounded by the River Wye to the west and with the Severn forming the long south-west to north-east hypotenuse. Lower ground, or perhaps even the A40 from Gloucester to Ross, provides the short northern edge. 'Of all Britain's ancient forests', says George Hill, 'Dean is the one which most closely fits the way we imagine a forest ought to look'. In fact the ancient wildwood itself was much changed by replanting in the last century and by the disastrous modern preference for conifers. For all that, it still feels like an ancient forest, not least because of the hilly terrain; wooded ridges seem to stretch in all directions. Its quiddity was guaranteed by the Norman kings who wanted good hunting grounds, but their successors were more interested in good timber for their fighting ships. This Royal Forest, though, was always to be as much defined by its industry as by its trees. These are carboniferous limestone hills rich in minerals; it was probably the Celts who first mined the iron ore with the Romans and Normans following suit; it was the Romans who first exploited the coal that lies above and within the iron. Industrial workers have always been different and in a very real sense the political identity of the Forest was established as early as the late thirteenth-century when the Free Miners, those born within the Forest and who had worked in an iron or coal mine for 366 days, were given certain rights with regard to workings.

Geology, geography and history have all combined to give the Forest a unique and fascinating history. The main roads quite clearly skirt it; one has to make a special effort to effect an entry and then, once on the inside, it is hardly surprising that one encounters distinctive political and cultural traditions. This is hardly the terrain for landowning aristocrats and gentry, and perhaps no area in the country was to be so free of their influence. Here foresters, miners and colliers were jealous of ancient rights and proud of that independence achieved in negotiation with the highest of authorities. It was an area ripe for Nonconformity, for radical liberals such as Sir Charles Dilke and for trade unionism. Everything pointed to the contrast with the rural shires to the north and west. Indeed things were different just twenty miles away, for in the most famous Gloucestershire autobiography ever written, *Cider with Rosie*, the poet Laurie Lee recalled that in the 1920s his village had 'revolved around the Squire'. Gloucestershire is an ancient and proud county and yet, as Humphrey Phelps stresses, no Forester will ever initially identify himself as coming from the county. In half an hour or so a Dean resident can be in the cathedral city of Gloucester, a place, says Potter, 'one would always want to get out of as quickly as possible'. To the west is Wales, and in particular the South Wales coalfield with its own more recent, more fervent and certainly more infamous traditions of militant independence, but no Forester will ever want to claim blood-brotherhood in that direction. Wales had its uses; there were jobs there that could be taken up in bad days, there was a beach and funfair at Barry Island and of course out of Wales would come choirs, bands and above all rugby teams that the Foresters would want to demolish in competition. But one must never forget that the Foresters are English, English in a very special way, patriotic (as Potter was often to emphasise) in ancient deep-rooted ways that depended little on what bosses and politicians thought to be the needs of the hour. They were naturally suspicious of Gloucester and even more so of London, and yet hated to have their stubbornness in any way associated with that of South Wales. 'Being ruled from Cardiff', says Potter, was one of the things miners hated about the standardisation that came after 1948. Phelps tells the marvellous tale of the Forester who lived less than two miles from the Welsh border and who was rung from Essex to be asked what the weather was like in Wales. 'I told him', said the Forester, 'that this was the Forest of Dean, not bloody Wales. That silly bugger thought he was speaking to a Welshman'. More often than not, of course, it is the accent that most sharply differentiates the Dean resident from his Welsh neighbour. Potter himself attributes something of the speed and lilt of local speech to Welsh influence but 'the broad, lengthened vowel sounds and buttery emphases' are very much of the West Country. Foresters, though, do not simply have the rural burr of those shires between London and Bristol, for unbroken traditions stretching back to pre-Norman times have combined with an intense Biblical schooling and industrial solidarity to produce a distinct vocabulary and what Potter identifies as distinctive rhythms.

In *The Changing Forest*, published in 1962, Potter conceded that the Forest proper was 'as beautiful surely as any place on earth'. He had found that the word 'idyllic' had 'irritatingly' kept intruding and finally had to be accepted. The Forest is indeed lovely, one of England's great surprises; to visit it even briefly is a refreshing experience that somehow restores one's increasingly shaken belief that there is such a country as England. One further surprise is that the great majesty of the Wye Valley and the beauty of the Forest is not matched by the area's small towns and villages. They are, as local writers like Phelps willingly admit, not particularly attractive. It takes wealth and authority to produce either urban or village style and that has not been the Forest's way. Undistinguished is the word that comes to mind. Coleford, the capital of West Dean, has a central Market Place from which busy streets head off in all directions: there is certainly a feeling of intimacy but no real sense of municipal purpose, no building seems related to any other. To the northwest the land climbs for a couple of miles and one comes to the village of Berry Hill, referred to sometimes by the less mellifluous but possibly more accurate term of Berry

Slope. Today this community is a pleasant and semi-rural mixture of rather nondescript housing and institutions forming a ribbon-like development along roads that come together at several cross-roads. There are picturesque cottages and one or two more solid artisans' homes, but they are intermingled now with council houses and with the newer pretentious bungalows and detached homes of those who have done well. The church is on the periphery; the chapels are more in the midst of things but look modest and rather forlorn. All the recreational buildings have a doll's house quality, although it looks as if the sportsfields offer by far the most important and perhaps the only flourishing local activity. What has gone from the Forest today is the old industry. There are certainly factories in the towns but what heavy industry there was, the mines and collieries that created the Berry Hills, have gone and with them their names: the Waterloo, the Northern, the Princess Royal and especially the Titanic, names chosen and then used with pride and awe.

The Forest has always been lovely but Potter has never claimed that quality for his particular part of it. There was nothing picturesque about the exceedingly plain Berry Hill house where he was born and brought up and where six people of three different generations shared two bedrooms and used an outside toilet. It was with some feeling that he was to quote D.H. Lawrence's famous denunciation of an ugly England with its 'ugly houses'. The sheer plainness and utilitarian ordinariness of such housing set just a few miles from the splendour of Symonds Yat would seem to predicate a duality of feeling and to an astonishing degree this divided aesthetic response to the Forest was to be a pattern repeated in his response to the world of his childhood generally. The loyalties are clear. The man who was thought to have ridiculed his parents on television takes care in *The Glittering Coffin* to reassert his pride and his debt. 'Thank God, however, my family is now closer than it was before — and it was a happy family then' is how he sums things up: we are not then to go down the Lawrentian or Osbornian roads of unhappy families. There is no sense of alienation but rather a gentle boasting of the extent to which he belongs. His wife is from Coleford, he still puts on the black-and-amber jersey of the local rugby team, still drinks as a regular at the pub and the club and still goes to the local Labour

Party meetings. His loyalties are personal and associational and they are also historic, for this is a community that has worked and has sustained real values. He was born in 1935, so his earliest memories are of the War years, and then his adolescence was to coincide with a period in which Potter thought the culture of the Forest could be seen at its fullest. These were years in which jobs and the Welfare State gave people the wherewithal and confidence to enjoy the old forms of recreation to the full; these were good years for the rugby teams, the chapels, the band, the carnival, the cinemas, the pubs and the organisers of charabanc outings. The Forest had real meaning in those days: it had possessed a working-class culture that had been deeply satisfying and which had given Potter a model and ideal he was never to abandon. It forms the crucial reference point in *The Glittering Coffin* and he ends *The Changing Forest* by returning to this set of values and activities and by virtually demanding that loyalty to it should not be 'abandoned' or written off.

It was a world, though, that Potter had at least in part left behind. Inevitably young people have to move away from their parents and out of their childhoods. What the undergraduate had found difficult to come to terms with (and hence his emergence as a writer) was the admission that in several ways he had wanted to establish himself in a new world. The real confessions in his early writing are to be found in the accumulated reservations with the culture in which he had been reared, for 'conformity is ... the most important feature of working-class life'. There is 'a stifling warmth' in all that 'associational life' and 'much of what is indiscriminately labelled "working-class" is hostile by definition to any form of progressive thought and is little but a narrow, bitterly defensive reaction to the abuses of capitalism, the consequence of stunted under-privilege rather than social vigour and optimism'. What this builds up to is the full admission that amidst what family rows there were, especially on a Saturday night 'when cider by the pint had sharpened the usual banter into something nearer to cruelty', and amidst the teasing and ragging that followed real achievement at school, there came the premonition that the familiar world could not deal with the degree of individuality he needed to assert. The young Potter needed to be free, and that is what Oxford promised. In *The Changing Forest* he recalled how the

Forest itself offered space to children who had felt 'the tightness and stifle of close identity' in the villages. There had been 'an insistent beat' to the sense of community, the way of life had been 'totally encompassing and occasionally imprisoning' and 'in the coils of intimacy ... much intolerance had been bred'. In his father's generation there had been 'a tremendously powerful clannishness' which had not yet broken down and that 'male-dominated society' had seemed 'alternatively amusing, irritating and admirable'.

It was surely these reservations that allowed the young author to realise that nostalgia was not to be his mode. Perhaps it seems remarkable that we even need to talk about nostalgia when looking at an author still in his mid-twenties. But, as we have seen, there were so many particular reasons why writers of this generation were aware of the worlds from which they had come. As early as his first book, though, Potter had realised that 'secondhand nostalgia is no aid to objectivity' and that in any case the mere exercise of academic or literary assessment represents 'a form of withdrawal'. The writer has necessarily become an outsider, removed not only from the family, the hearth and the community but also from the being that had been himself as a child. The new feeling that 'my boyhood belongs to someone else' was part of the very tension that was generating ambition and unleashing talent. At a surprisingly early and highly advantageous stage in his writing career Potter had established what his relationship would be with his past. It was there to be used when he needed its truths: there was no need to renounce it, ask favours because of it or to idealise it for any crude political purpose.

To reread Dennis Potter's first two books thirty years on is a fascinating exercise, and so far we have been chiefly noting those remarks and observations that hint at his subsequent literary identity. In his later assessment of those works he quite rightly stressed the extent to which they were very much occasioned by the immediate concerns of the late 1950s. Inevitably students of the late Potter are drawn to the psychological insights and to the way in which the collier's son became the Oxford undergraduate. But in fact the main theme of both books was the extent to which England as a whole and the Forest of Dean in particular were changing in the face of a new commercialism and consumerism heavily dependent on advertising and television. Like so many contemporary writers he was concerned to defend what he thought of as traditional English values against the onslaught of what was essentially an Americanisation of the country. It is this theme which so often makes him sound like both Richard Hoggart and John Osborne. The writing in this vein is not surprisingly of less interest today than his more personal revelations; there are perhaps too many references to jukeboxes and the new music — for surely every generation is entitled to define its own musical styles — and his countless somewhat sneering remarks about 'neat suburbia', 'suburban hedgerows', 'privet hedges' and 'well-mannered conversation over garden fences' seem obsessive. The books are full of snappy and flashy phrases which contemptuously discuss the new economy of the Macmillan era. He saw that era as being characterised by a kind of glittering but hollow expresso-bar prosperity'; 'the Coca-Cola onslaught of the New World' had created a 'synthetic Madison Avenue concocted way of life 'dominated by 'the chiming cash registers of the new chain stores'. His words convey the strength of feeling but the power is that of prejudice rather than of social evaluation. There is no suggestion here that living standards were in fact higher than ever before and that much of the 'ugliness' of the thirties and austerity of the forties were disappearing. So much of what was acquired and consumed is for him merely junk and he rejects any new social analysis which offered grateful thanks for washing-machines and hairdryers. He believes that 'the dignity of ordinary people is being swamped by the forces of admass', but one suspects he has arrived at that conclusion less because he has actually seen it happen than because he believed 'almost all the mass media' to be 'in the control of eager, criminally commercial outside hands'.

The England of Harold Macmillan was indeed a new country and Dennis Potter just did not like it. That, of course, is the real trouble of these early books for so much of the effective writing reflected what could only have been a personal dislike of new modes and of commercial innovation. If nostalgia was no basis for literature, neither could it be for politics. Potter had conceived of *The Glittering Coffin* as something of a political manifesto, and yet in the strictest sense it was hardly a political book at all. In the fullest review that the book received, and it was one that Potter much appreciated, Richard Wollheim argued that it was surely 'unjust to call our speculation about society and culture "political" until we have worked our way back from the more imaginative vision to some suggestion, however fragmentary, of how the vision can be realized'. Basically Potter's position in his first two books was that things in the country are not as they were in the Forest of Dean in the 1940s and that, of course, is a conservative stance that could lead nowhere. All the time he generalises from the experience of the Forest (he still knows only the Forest, Oxford and London) and he takes Cinderford's 'sprawling mediocrity' to be typical of the nation as a whole. On television the glossy biscuit adverts look fine but at that company's Cinderford factory where he had worked for three months wage rates were low, there were no unions and workers headed straight for the cafe with its jukebox. All over the Forest the pits were closing and now the author's father, having spent a lifetime working underground, found himself in his fifties having to take a boring irksome job as a bus cleaner at the garage in Coleford. This is highly relevant material, a much needed corrective to Conservative Party propaganda, but it is never evaluated in any wider political or economic context. With his personal feelings and when describing his own career Potter had achieved a scrupulous balance and detachment which he did not employ when describing mere social change.

For all the phrase-making and special-pleading there are moments of real insight in this early Potter, and occasionally he sounds as if he was penning his social critique in 1990 rather than in 1960. Clearly we can label him a premature anti-Thatcherite not least when he warns that 'the sovereignty of the consumer is a phrase that reeks of dishonesty' and pleads for that and other advertising cant to be confined to the 'museum of myths and propaganda'. Already, a generation before it was to become the chief Thatcher slogan, Potter knew the possible deception involved in offering people 'a choice', for "choice" can be imposed or offered in all sorts of loaded ways. Similarly he realised that an apparent "freedom of opportunity" could be largely spurious and was indeed resulting in some cases in a 'hardening of class lines'. One can fault his refusal to face up to the economic and psychological realities of consumerism and suggest that it was his puritanism that prejudiced him against the sheer fun, flair and opportunity that both advertising and new marketing techniques had generated. Clearly, though, it was his writer's ear, trained by hours of listening to the terse realism of colliers, to the radio and to preachers, that allowed him to spot the manipulation of a new rhetoric that suggested that affluence would come easily to all and pretended that no special care or attention was needed as older safeguards and constraints were removed. He had noticed in particular the new emphasis on the word "youth". Right across the board of consumer interests salesmen, agents, retailers, advertisers and journalists did all they could to promote and exploit that whole new range of young customers, whereas for the respectable and especially the ageing the country's "youth" had already been identified as a problem. With real insight the Oxford man could see that he had done well to get out of the Forest but for those left behind and for those who could not excel in school things were not going to be so easy. In *The Changing Forest* Potter was opening up a debate on the fate of 'the pop generation' in an age of de-industrialisation that was not to become fashionable for another twenty years.

His analysis of the young people of Dean leads to the most remarkable and important sentence in the book. Potter had noticed that 'anything which is collective in the old ways, that smacks of ponderous and too-nostalgic talk on the themes of "a sense of community" is associated with the drab and the second-rate'. Here the writer tells as much about himself as about the Forest as he reveals precisely why he was worried about the way in which the country was moving away from his 1940s model of what it should be. There is much that can be said about the second half of this key sentence, but only after we have noted the use of the politically emotive word "collective" in the initial phrase. The most obvious collective effort in the Forest of Potter's childhood and adolescence was the Labour Movement. He had become conscious of society at the very same time as that Movement was achieving real power and implementing many of the schemes of which the Dean colliers had long dreamed. In so many ways Labour and the Unions had contributed to that fullness of a culture that had characterized Potter's 1940s. And yet throughout these two books conceived at the end of the fifties he never misses a chance to score a point off the Labour Movement and to accuse it of having betrayed its loyal supporters. He wants a 'radical' party that 'should splutter with life and polemic' but sees a Labour Party that had 'never been so distant from the enthusiasm, hopes, aspirations of its youngest members'. For him Mr Gaitskell was as much a 'fun-fair barker' as Macmillan, and even Mr Bevan seemed to be surrendering his distinctive voice as he accepted the bipartisan necessity of ensuring Britain maintained its Cold War stance. The proletariat seemed as far removed as ever from having any real control of their lives, not least because the leaders of the 'Judas' TUC had one eye on their future visit to Buckingham Palace. In *The Changing Forest* he was more specific and more personal. For years the colliers of the Forest had fought for nationalisation but when it had come it had resulted in pit closures and a loss of local control. With obvious empathy he reports on how the new influence of Cardiff (presumably in respect of both the NCB and the Union) is held to be responsible for the dramatic shrinking of the Forest coalfield. What had been heralded as a new age for miners had for the Forest turned out to be very much a mixed blessing; there was a new antipathy to Wales and Potter now relished the chance to air it. He was writing at the time of Bevan's death and at the very moment when the Welsh politician was being hailed by many intellectuals as the greatest of Labour's leaders; but Potter, as the son of a Dean collier, has no reservations in recalling Nye's admission in 1959 that some pits would have to be closed. As far as this aspect of collective effort is concerned the author knows of what he speaks and again public rhetoric and mythology must be made subservient to the personal experience. Presumably the young Labour Party hopeful with potential Cabinet credentials thought there was no harm in drawing attention to himself by speaking out against all and sundry. But there was an edge to his anti-Labourism that suggests that he was not destined to figure prominently, if at all, in this collectivist party. The hierarchy of loyalties that emerge from his accounts of personal experience would already point to the anarchism of the writer rather than the acquiescence of the party politician.

At this stage in his career the fundamental loyalty was to community and it was in this respect that the threat to what was "collective" worried Potter most. As far as the Forest was concerned his fear and regret was that everything public and commu-

nal was running down, that things that once brought people
together to fight, to play, to amuse, whether it be rugby, the union,
the carnival, the band, were now thought of as 'drab and second-
rate'. Even conversation and communication had been affected;
talk seemed 'second-hand', 'the animation of the old culture has
dwindled away'. Community was being eroded in the Forest and
yet this concept, this sense of what his village had been like in the
1940s has now become his model, his ideal for the country as a
whole. That quite simply is the message of his first two books. His
argument is always that we must avoid nostalgia but whenever
he wants to clinch his argument that the Britain of the late 1950s
was 'dead', 'an old man's land', 'a dead land, grey in its values,
ambitions and pleasures', the comparison that is made is with the
Forest he remembers. His touchstone is always those qualities he
admired in the Forest where people were on the whole working-
class but where society was 'practically speaking classless': 'everybody speaks in the street, without any cap-touching'. Most people
too were 'profoundly community-conscious'. For all the regretted
changes and the erosion of the forties' level of participation the
one thing that encourages Potter is that in the Forest at least
something of the old spirit lingers on; there was some resistance.
He was 'struck by the ways, the scores of deliberate ways, by
which people stand aside or despise the commercial standards of
this present society, by the multitude of commercial associations
and the strength of the loyalties within them'. He had found 'some
degree of conscious opposition to the economic benefits of central-
ization and mobility' and clearly this was something that those in
rebellion like himself, whether in the Labour Party or intellectual
circles, had to recognise and build on. That was really the only
hope. There was 'force' and 'vitality' in this 'heritage', some
indeed of which was reflected in 'pop culture', and the need now
was to come to terms with these things and see them as a central
ingredient of the national culture, or what in later years Potter was
to call 'the common culture'.

In both books Potter directs his anger at those forces which deny
the vitality of what Hoggart had described as 'the all-pervading
working-class culture'. His most spectacular tirades are against
the ad-men and the values of Coca-Cola and the women's magazines, but he is pretty hostile too towards the leaders of British

society, those groups who constituted 'the Establishment' and whose offspring he first encountered at Oxford. It is their clinging to the past, to Britain's imperial grandeur and Cold War militarism which prevented them from having any real interest in domestic, social and cultural values. They were, of course, totally dismissive of working-class culture, and it was precisely their clinging to a 'high culture' which they thought of as exclusively theirs and standing in sharp contrast to the lowness of working-class culture that gave the ad-men the freedom to step in and exploit the masses. The hallmark of this élite was its self-satisfaction, its total conformity within its own set of values and its definition of natural identity exclusively in terms of a nostalgia for an England in its own image. These are the people quite content to let the blood run out of everything Potter took to be the basis of English identity, pride and patriotism as long as they could maintain all the vital distinctions, that 'constant rhythm of class' that defined their way of life and guaranteed their standard of living. In the whole university at Oxford he had not found one person who seemed 'able or willing to make the leap from the atmosphere and petty conflicts of the senior common-room to a positive engagement with the realities involved in adapting a consistent, comprehensive and vital attitude to modern society'. This, of course, was exactly what he was now setting out to do.

What needed more precise definition was the exact sphere in which Potter himself would become engaged. His background and education had given him many options; the rugby-playing son of a coalminer and trade unionist who had gone on to be a prominent journalist, Labour activist, university debater and drama enthusiast would seem to be qualified for a whole range of careers that were opening up in the Britain of the day. What is interesting at this stage, however, is the extent to which Potter was very much an intellectual of his time. In true 1950s style his argument against "the Establishment" is sustained not in economic or political but rather cultural terms. The vital evidence for Britain's mediocrity or 'death' was to be found in the way in which the ruling elite's narrow definition of culture had cut off primarily the cinema and theatre but also journalism from vast tracts of social reality and many processes of social change. It was in this revealing and decisive area of culture that the country's submission to the 'ascendancy of the aristocracy and gentry' was most clearly evident. The assumption running right through Potter's two books of social observation was that cultural life in Britain had to be opened up so as to allow for the kind of participation and enthusiasm that had characterized the working-class culture of his youth. This,of course, was standard Hoggart-Williams orthodoxy, the position defined subsequently by Alan Sinfield as 'Left-Culturalism', the notion that cultural transformation to be effected in terms of new kinds of books, films and plays would somehow overthrow the "Establishment" and allow democratic fulfilment. As Sinfield suggests, the emergence of what was often thought of as a specifically class struggle for the culture of Britain in the 1950s is one of those vital clues that reveals so much about the difficulty of effecting real political change in a country where politicians take care to isolate themselves from many aspects of the national life. He points, too, to the extent to which what some thought of as a vital moment of cultural possibility inevitably generated a degree of rhetoric, pretension and myth. For all the talk and hype the actual level of accomplishment was low; books, plays and films could shock but there was no inherent value in kitchen-sink or mill-town settings. With hindsight we can see that what the cultural battle was really about was working-class, or rather regional, energy. Talented people with new voices were just asking to be given a chance and in general the sense of crisis that they helped generate (aided as always, as Marwick stresses, by the media) allowed them that chance. Across the culture, in theatres, in studios, in senior common rooms, in publishing houses, Dennis Potters were being given their chance. That did not necessarily mean that 'the ascendancy of the aristocracy and the gentry' was being overthrown. The Dennis Potters of the time were given their voice, they were pushing at half-opened doors, but their quite justifiable sense of being pioneers prevented them from seeing that it was their individual talent and energy that had taken them to prominence, not the qualities of the working-class culture on whose behalf they had called for a transformation. It took a little while for them to see that their own careers were as much a contribution to the decline of working-class culture as the forces of Coca-Cola.

The arts as such were not to be greatly transformed as a result of all that heated debate in the 1950s. Many of those who saw class as the great obstacle to artistic excellence in Britain were incapable of understanding that it was to be the dreaded phenomena of popular music and advertising that were to be far more potent and creative forces in the culture than film or theatre. In a quieter way, however, spectacular victories were to be won, victories that ensured that the values that Potter and others so closely associated with the working-class community of the 1940s were to have an institutional base that allowed them to flourish for another generation. The Hoggart-Williams revolution really succeeded above all in education where the advent of social scientists and primarily social historians radically shifted the curriculum away from the nineteenth century public-school model and rooted it far more decisively in the working-class culture of their own childhood. Nostalgia for working-class community became one of the hallmarks of a social-science or arts education in Britain and the books that had been shaped by the individual experiences of writers in the 1950s became the textbooks of a new politics. In one of the great ironies of British social history the new educationalists conspired in the destruction of the grammar school, the one institution that had allowed children like Dennis Potter to go to Oxford with the ability and confidence to take on the "Establishment" on their own terms. This was the greatest price that had to be paid for a politics defined exclusively in terms of culture and social envy rather than in more general economic terms.

The other Hoggart-Williams victory came in the sphere of broadcasting. Here the unique public corporation status of the BBC, the fact that commercial television was introduced in the crucial decade of the 1950s and was subject to political instruction to reflect both the artistic and regional vitality of the nation, taken with the heavy recruitment into broadcasting of university arts graduates, ensured a far greater influence for contemporary intellectual ideas than could possibly be the case with film or theatre where self-made entrepreneurs guaranteeed the resilience of commercial values. Only slowly, however, did the realisation develop that broadcasting was there to be taken; for a while the dangers were more apparent, all the advantages seemed to belong to various enemies. BBC Radio, of course, had its own place in that working-class culture of blessed memory. Its tunes, its voices, its laughter had been very much part of the home, its programmes had structured the day almost as definitively as work and leisure routines, in time of war it had articulated a sense of national identity, and its music and catch-phrases had gradually edged into a position alongside sport and rather ahead of religion as a mainstay of working-class discourse. And yet, for all that, radio did not really belong to the people. There was a democracy to its music and its humour but they came as part of a carefully controlled package. 'I know', said Potter in *The Glittering Coffin*, 'that the BBC is considered as an extension of the "Them"'. As far as both radio and television were concerned Potter conceded that the BBC 'attempts to make points of contact' but that it could never really escape its class base. It was rooted in what was thought of as a 'superior culture', inevitably it patronized the people as it condescended to reach out to them rather in the way of any wealthy do-gooder. What was crucially revealing for this son of Dean was the way in which the BBC ran quite distinct radio networks for different audiences, for the total separation of Light and Third programme audiences was seen as a negation of what working-class community stood for.

Potter conceded that the advent of a commercial rival had made the BBC a little less stuffy but that was no compensation for greater dangers. All the signs were that television would now be totally taken over by the advertisers and the promoters of the pop culture, and often he seemed to be suggesting that television sets would just become a development from the dreaded jukebox. Here was the instrument that would ensure the final obliteration of that 1940s world. It was the tricks and wiles of advertisers that would 'impose' the popularity of ITV's inferior programmes, that would ensure the triumph of the commercial over the 'genuine' and contribute to the way in which Britain was being made into a shoddier version of America. It was ITV that was guaranteeing the triumph of the 'telly' and in *The Changing Forest* Potter lined up his adjectives to sum up what the 'telly' amounted to. It was 'dreary, repetitive, sordid, commercial and second-rate'. Throughout the book he keeps on indicating the insidious tactics of the enemy that had come from outside and was now living amongst his people. In the Berry Hill pub a miner is talking about 1926, but a line of another conversation intrudes, a female voice of course: 'I like that

Hughie Green on the telly — he's so sincere!' In the club there is a twenty-one inch screen on a corner shelf. The phrase 'smokey-grey face' is used to suggest its human potency as the representation in their midst of an alien agency. The early works of Dennis Potter are shot through with irony, not least in the instance of that twenty-one inch television set. The evil eye of the Madison Avenue gods it may have seemed but it was also to be the vehicle of fame of the man who was destined to become the Forest of Dean's most famous son. Even as readers acquainted themselves with the Berry Hill Workingmen's Club the members would have already seen themselves in the original television programme and soon they were to see actors playing them in a fictional version of the Club. It was on its way to becoming the best known working-men's club in the land, it was becoming part of the national culture.

Certainly in these social and cultural tracts Potter had been shuffling the cards that were being dealt by the formative writers and teachers of the decade. We would do him a grave injustice if we took them at face value as a major critique of the nation. Essentially they are journalistic essays, albeit ones that deserve to be reissued and reread every bit as much as some of the slight novels and plays of the 1950s that have worked their way both on to every syllabus and to the bookshelf of every graduate of the time. They nicely convey the preoccupations of the period. They give firm evidence of the new energy that was gurgling up from the provinces as well as indicating precisely those areas of the culture in which those energies would be expressed. The prejudices and misconceptions they reveal were to blight British life for a generation and were to serve to confirm ideological political divisions at the very time when they were becoming futile. Yes, there had been an alternative and vibrant working-class culture in the 1940s but that had been predicated by economic circumstances that could not endure. Yes, there were starkly contrasting cultural differences between working-class and upper-class lifestyles, and yet to sum up society as a whole on the basis of that judgement was perhaps a little naive. As Potter himself conceded there was an unattractive intolerance in working-class circles but even more fundamentally, as Wollheim argued, there were far more than two cultural patterns in the land:

a truer model would be one that pointed to many overlapping and mutually interacting sub-cultures. Inevitably sub-cultures develop their own vocabulary and style and, again as Wollheim argued, much of what critics like Potter took to be class was rather a question of 'snobbery'. Adults can choose what they want to be, opt for conformity or rebellion or in most cases a formal amalgam in which integrity rests on both loyalty and adaptation. In journalistic and even scholarly accounts far too much is made of externals: accents are not necessarily the man and a bottle of claret need not be a class statement. Potter could jeer at middle-class journalists watching an arts discussion on the BBC Monitor programme with 'chinking light refracted through brandy glasses' without realising the extent to which his future career would be largely defined at that particular nexus of the culture.

Above all the Hoggart-Williams-Potter school failed to understand the nature of aspiration in the new consumer age. Even in the old working-class culture there had been far more choice than social critics would admit. There were many ways of being different even if opting for bay windows, flower gardens, Anglicanism, fancy waistcoats or facial hair hardly seemed like freedom to a later generation. Patterns of behaviour and consumption were changing but in regretting a new commercialism and new marketing techniques Potter and the others were pouring scorn on precisely those developments which were doing most to release people from the drabness of the past. There would be far greater differences between people who were near neighbours but there would be infinitely more room for self-expression and fulfilment. Just as many fifties writers failed to see that the most significant cultural aspect of the decade was precisely the new freedom they had won for themselves so they failed to appreciate the new economic opportunities that were opening up at all levels of society and not least for working-class families. Conditions now allowed for individual taste and style and for many people privet hedges represented both real achievement and aesthetic preference. It was not only academic success or literary fame which were taking people away from 'the thousands of streets with hop-scotch marks on the pavements and chalk or whitewash scribblings on the walls'. The Dennis Potter of 1960 thought that 'class matters more than it did in 1945'. Historians must conclude that it was awareness of class, the discussion of class, that mattered most in 1945. That was the case because things were now changing rapidly in the lives of working-class youths who had been success- ful at school. Class was a feature of the national debate in the late fifties because many people were now crossing those 'contour lines' of class that Potter thought could so easily be plotted on the map. Some people crossed those lines more easily and with fewer regrets than others but what was remarkable was the extent to which a nostalgia for hop-scotch marks on the pavement seemed particularly prevalent amongst intellectuals and writers and be- came the subject of their work and the basis of their radical politics. There was certainly to be an audience and a readership for their work and nostalgia was soon to develop into the preferred na- tional mode, though the masses seemed rather less inclined to let sentiment for the past affect their political choice. It really did appear to be the case that a breed of writers and academics had a special need to attach themselves to the world that had just been lost.

This was certainly the first sense in which class was to matter for Dennis Potter. First as a young teenager and then again at twenty-one he had been taken away from the Forest of Dean, a world that for all its shortcomings now seemed classless, honest, direct and fulfilling. Like so many other intellectuals of his gener- ation his Socialism really amounted to a wish that those conditions could be replicated nationally. He appeared to become less of a political writer but throughout the decades ahead he would sum up his social views by reiterating his belief in the quasi-political concept of a 'common culture'. His recollection of the Forest of his childhood always fired his strong conviction that however cyni- cally advertisers and broadcasters targeted sections as groups and however decisively and irrevocably educationists isolated élites there was in essence one greatly underestimated intelligent, thor- oughly worthwhile, mass audience. This was undoubtedly the strongest legacy from the Forest and from those years at Oxford when he had been encouraged to contemplate class. As was not uncommon amongst writers of his generation he was to retain political and cultural values that had been defined in the 1940s even as he took advantage of the new freedoms and opportunities that affluence allowed. Generally, as we have seen, it was the twin agencies of academe and television that were to allow this quite decisive cultural configuration by attracting and promoting writers and thinkers of Potter's disposition. Now, as his first books were published, Potter had left the university and had commenced what was to be an enduring association with television. Inevitably chance played a part in that development but undoubtedly his views on class and culture had made him a natural for British television.

That is not all there is to be said about Dennis Potter and class, for his interest in it goes beyond his belief in a common culture. The dimension of class was to be present in many of his plays and increasingly some critics came to see it as a preoccupation. This was especially the case with his depiction of affluent life-styles; Clive James was to suggest that it seemed to be the author's position that wherever there was a middle-class family it needed to be shaken up. The privet hedge had gone on being a clue to his anger. There are moments, certainly, when we can see Potter giving vent to a somewhat gratuitous class prejudice and merely illustrating, if nothing else, that writers (like other people) just have straightforward class preferences. But there is more to it than that. As he became a less political writer so he returned to the personal truths that had been included almost as asides in his earlier sociological writing. Class was important now not so much as the launchpad of a political career in which he led the downtrodden but rather because it had happened to him, it had been experienced. Class distinction, snobbery if you like, could hurt and all the wounds inflicted did not immediately go away. The miners of Dean had been clannish but then had come the discovery that all groups are clannish; they all tend to ridicule the exotic accent and the strange vocabulary. There were new freedoms but also betrayals of trust. Groups of the talented and favoured wanted to be exclusive and to claim privilege but that nearly always involved degrees of hypocrisy. They had an ability to change the rules, to devise their own rules, and so were able to side-step many of the anxieties and even tragedies that characterised working-class life. They were very different, these people; they were indeed the inhabitants of a different country and perhaps needed to be shaken up. Later it would often be asked whether Potter was a Marxist. He was to deny the label but was to confess that he accepted certain Marxist evaluations, not least the sense of being 'conned and cheated'. There is always in Potter a sense that the workingclass do not have access to some middle-class secrets.

Crossing class boundaries is something that most people have to take in their stride but that was not the case with Dennis Potter. His own sense of unease and anger was picked up by a television reporter and then further embarrassment was caused by the inter-vention of the press. So written explanations had been called for. The problem was a rational or cultural one — or was it? All the while political, personal and literary considerations were criss-crossing and so it was that class was present at the conception and birth of the writer. His preoccupations were to change, as indeed was his own lifestyle, but there was always to be that edge of bitterness and anger that had first emerged as he realised that everything that was most personal and private could be cruelly exposed at the very instant that class identity was probed. Class was not merely a badge or a football club banner that could be picked up when convenient, for it could be that it defined or constrained personality in much deeper ways. Potter now turned from the great social battle of class to consider the more immediate and dramatic battles of individual characters who would be con-cerned with fulfilment of aspirations, with weakness, guilt, belief or sex. But over and over again as he traced these dilemmas he was finding it necessary and useful to deploy the essential, and not merely external, dimensions of class. For the writer whose sense of class had been at its sharpest at the very moment that he first understood the nature of his own talent it became the natural thing to stress not so much the political but rather the psychologi-cal truths of class.

A Life In Television

Christopher Mayhew's question about class had heralded what for Dennis Potter was to be a lengthy connection with television. By the time *The Glittering Coffin* was published the Oxford graduate was working for BBC Television's Current Affairs Department and by the time the themes he had raised in his programme *Between Two Rivers* had been developed in his second book, *The Changing Forest*, he had moved on to become one of the country's pioneering television critics working for *The Daily Herald*. He was working as a journalist and still doing some television criticism when his first plays began to appear on the small screen. For twenty-five years thereafter writing for television was his chief preoccupation and the result was a long list of plays many of which were to be the subject of national debate and several of which were immediately identified, not least by the most respected Fleet Street critics, as being amongst the medium's crowning achievements.

The praise from critics such as Philip Purser and Richard Last must be particularly gratifying for Potter. Purser, of course, was to do more than just draw attention to Potter, for his 1981 article on the television plays was the first real assessment of the work and in a sense it established both the reputation of the playwright and the medium itself not to mention the very practice of television criticism. It has been Purser, too, who has gone on reminding people that Potter himself had been an early and important writer on television; he has done this whilst he explains to a later generation the highly distinctive and influential concept of television that a small circle of Fleet Street critics, including both Potter and himself, had shared. It had not been easy for those first critics to establish the credentials of their new profession, one that they

44

generally believed to have been invented by Peter Black of *The Daily Mail*. By the end of the 1950s the evidence was suggesting that the readers of morning newspapers wanted to see some considered comment on their previous evening's viewing and so the convention emerged of television columns in which critics would present their individual reactions in such a way as to amuse, reassure and possibly challenge. One problem, of course, was that every viewer was an expert on television and instinctively felt superior to the critic; and the other was that, given the widespread assumption that both television and journalism only merited immediate consumption, it was doubly true of television criticism that it was eminently disposable. It was a modest enough job that nobody took seriously and that many actually despised. It was generally assumed that those selected had drawn the short straws: one of the victims, Byron Rogers of *The Sunday Times*, described it as 'a form of house arrest'. There were so many factors in Fleet Street that buttressed the time-honoured conventions that journalists never became academic, theoretical or pretentious in their approach and this, it seemed, would above all apply to the new phenomenon of television reviewing. And yet against all the odds serious television reviewing began to emerge.

'A few of us', Philip Purser was later to recall, 'really did have, in those front-line days, a sense of playing a part in a battle that might go either way'. The issue to be decided was whether television would 'unite all classes, all brow-levels, all quarters of the kingdom in a common culture unknown since Shakespeare's day' or whether it would rather 'settle for the easy division'. This group of critics took their inspiration from the BBC itself which had been shaped by a history of at first running the one and only television channel, then by having to compete with a more popular commercial channel and finally by being given a second channel which was initially conceived of as catering for minority tastes.

Circumstances and tradition combined at the BBC to sustain a notion of planned and mixed viewing in which as large and as natural an audience as possible would be persuaded to accept an evening package in which music-hall comedy and entertainment would lead on to serious drama and current affairs analysis. As Purser understood it, the job of critics like Potter and himself was to do everything possible to ensure that quality programmes kept their place in the listings and that every encouragement was given to the best writers and programme-makers to find their own niche in the medium. 'As a critic,' he recalls, 'you cheered on all that was good and honest, and tried to expose all that was shoddy and calculated'.

Dennis Potter was very much part of this process. Perhaps it was inevitable that his own career at the BBC was short-lived as he could never be allowed to speak as freely on air as he had in the pages of *The New Statesman* and *The Glittering Coffin*. Deployment as a television critic was perhaps another inevitable development once he was in Fleet Street although it was to be the onset of his illness that made this the most obvious way for him to write for the papers. It was partly chance, then, and partly the nature of his politics that had concentrated his mind on television and allowed him fully to understand the extent to which it was of crucial importance in his scheme of things. He was from the outset a champion of television as an agent of 'the common culture' and it was only to be after two decades that his belief in the medium faltered. To an extent that was almost unique for somebody who was not actually fully employed as a broadcasting bureaucrat, he was to retain a belief in television's mission. He proudly informed an American critic that 'we take television more seriously here' and one is tempted to say that it is difficult to think of anyone here who has taken it more seriously than he has. When he was a critic, he explains, 'I used to get very angry about the pap' and that anger was fully justified given the importance of the medium. There was a time later when he was writing for television that he even confessed to having a certain empathy with Mary Whitehouse, the campaigner against permissive television, for at least she helped initiate debate and discussion. By the end of the seventies his complaint was that 'people don't care enough about television'. He cared about it most because it gave access to a uniquely national audience and he was always to be loath to join the rank of novelists and West End playwrights who were inevitably turning their backs on huge sections of the country. From the early days of television criticism he recalled the phrase that 'dons and coal-miners could well be watching'. The relevance of that reflection to his own career and politics is very obvious and although he came to think of it as a 'naive and patronising' remark it remained the inspiration of his television writing. Purser was to evoke the name of Shakespeare, and Potter that of Dickens whom he thought of as having displayed a confidence in a common culture by opting for the serial form. Potter too wanted to reach out to a mass audience not just to entertain but to challenge, to offer them a complex statement that he was sure they would comprehend. It was not an easy medium and he was never to claim that it was. It had strange powers which could easily be misused and for the well-intentioned the challenge and disciplines were formidable. It could be all or nothing, it could blur the senses, it was 'an occupying presence' in every home and nobody given access to it should accept the responsibility lightly. Nobody came to television with a fuller sense of expectation or duty than Dennis Potter. His beliefs as well as fate had taken him to that place in the culture.

His output was to be staggering. His twenty-five television plays represent one of the most considerable personal investments made in the medium and it is not difficult to see that in part he was inspired by his evangelical concept of it. He talks about television, as about almost everything else, in a very personal way, as if the responsibility on both sides is one of personal integrity and honour; again the vocabulary and terms of reference tend to be emotive and direct. In this respect we see how inevitable it was that he should move away somewhat from the other disciples of the Hoggart-Williams school. From the outset his expectations of the culture and of television had been couched in personal terms and what mattered more than anything was that he be allowed to communicate with an audience. Once he had established that drama was to be his mode his view of television became less political and academic. In the aftermath of Hoggart, and more especially Williams, a concern for the role of television became a defining characteristic of several different spheres of academic life in Britain, and there can be no other country in the world where histories or other studies of contemporary cultural developments are so dominated by an analysis of television. The pattern was to culminate in the emergence of a new academic discipline called Cultural Studies which on the basis of its most highly publicised text books would seem to be almost exclusively concerned with television. Here, too, we see something of that caring about television that Potter had called for and yet the concern was really quite different; and so, not surprisingly, very little of this new writing is devoted to Potter, the author that less academic critics have identified as television's greatest. It is fascinating to trace the process whereby he became somewhat marginalised in the output of academe. In part considerations were political, for left-wing writers were meant to write plays of political indignation in which the evils of class suppression were dramatized. In that respect the heroes were to be Jim Allen and Trevor Griffiths. What were needed were shocks to bourgeois complacency and here the main agent of change had been Ken Loach. In terms of drama the real achievement had been that of naturalism, first in individual plays and then in series. Real excitement was generated when a full sense of regional society could be captured within a popular format. Increasingly, serialised stories centred on crime and policing and these seemed fully to satisfy critics, academics and the masses. Eventually there were to be soap operas which not only became the most popular programmes on television but also those likely to occasion true ecstasy amongst academics who had now turned their backs on quality or difficult television and whose concept of a common culture seemed exclusively concerned with the interaction between fictional characters in undemanding series and the various sections of the mass audience. All this was far removed from Potter's sense of television and one senses that the spiritual descendant of the Hoggart-Williams revolution has for quite a time been as embarrassed by his plays as the supporters of Mary Whitehouse. Potter has played very little part in the way that the British have made television comfortable to live with or with the way the country's academics have divorced television criticism and analysis from any real discussion of what is serious and challenging. His perception of television is immensely personal and his work remains highly differentiated from the normal output.

From the outset the programme planners had wanted serious drama to be the cornerstone of their effort to guarantee the quality and distinctiveness of British television. Extremely worthy and often rather gloomy plays had been put out live throughout the 1950s, most often on Sundays evenings, a very appropriate time for high seriousness. All the while new acting techniques were emerging and eventually new technologies ended the necessity of broadcasting live from a studio; actors would no longer have to perspire. And so it was by the early 1960s that television drama was far more able to tackle the dramatic themes suggested by a rapidly changing society. The fairly regular diet of weekly plays had become television's probably most controversial and widely debated feature. The opportunities were there for new writers and it was an obvious chance for socially mobile writers to make their impact. For planners and critics alike the new drama was television at its best and yet, as Potter was later to reflect, the culture as a whole was slower to grant any status to this new and quite glittering branch of the literary profession. "Television" in front of the noble old word "Playwright", he was to reflect, is not entirely dissimilar to placing "processed" right next to "cheese"; and yet George Brandt could quote Harold Pinter's reflection that the audience for his television play *A Night Out* was equivalent in number to what a play in the theatre would take thirty years to accumulate. There was high praise for the new television playwrights but they were never regarded as agents in the culture in the way of Pinter, Osborne and Wesker, let alone novelists like Amis. They were thought of rather as journeymen because, of course, they were working within the overall format of popular television. Many of the best writers who worked for television were quite prepared to accept the humility and even the anonymity that the mores of the medium imposed, almost in the same way that the brilliantly talented directors of television commercials had to accept that their fame would be confined to their colleagues. The high profile of the *avant-garde* West End writers contrasted sharply with the modesty of television writers like Peter Nichols, David Mercer and Alan Plater. From the beginning, though, that was not quite Potter's way. The former television current affairs employee and outspoken journalist had launched his London career on the basis of direct speaking and confrontation and it was in that mood that he turned to what unsuspectedly was to be his new calling.

Why did he become a television playwright rather than any other kind of writer? Philip Purser reports that he was writing a novel which was abandoned in favour of more immediate results. Was that already because the onset of illness had made the sheer physical demand of the larger form more difficult? One obvious source of inspiration was the experience gained as a sketch writer for the very successful television satire show *That Was The Week That Was* and in fact his early plays were in part extended sketches written in the satirical mode and very much concerned with the themes he had treated in the Saturday night show. His first play *The Confidence Course*, broadcast in February 1965, debunked the promotional methods and rationale of salesmen offering ambitious yet nervous recruits a course in confidence building and personality development. By now Potter had worked in television and Fleet Street and he had seen at close quarters the new avenues that were opening up for slick promotional techniques and yet it was only when he began to write more directly out of his own experiences that he was more widely recognised as an interesting writer. A third play *Cinderella* did not get beyond the script stage and the next play *Vote, Vote, Vote for Nigel Barton* was held back for script changes and so was not broadcast until after its companion piece *Stand Up, Nigel Barton*. Potter was later to write about the need for any writer to find a voice and it was certainly in the Nigel Barton plays that we can hear that voice and identify the themes and techniques that were to become hallmarks. It was with those two plays that he really entered the national consciousness as a distinctive angry young talent who was going to assail viewers in a highly individualistic way. The power of both plays undoubtedly came from their directly autobiographical inspiration. *Barton* is obviously a version of Potter at two very crucial moments in the author's own career and yet one senses that the highly personal issues could now be broached in this way because of his confidence that the plays would be accepted and would work in their own way. He was later to make the point that he wrote "drama" rather than prose fiction 'precisely to avoid the question "Who is saying this?"' This explanation can only be accepted as a personal insight rather than literary criticism for quite obviously natural novelists have not had that much difficulty in distancing themselves from first-person heroes. What Potter is revealing is that he, as the author of two works of polemical prose in which personal experience had served as inspiration, had needed to devise distancing techniques. A range of characters, a blend of techniques and a mixing of modes gave him the complexity he needed and encouraged him to probe those crucial moments in his own life that he needed to understand more fully. The play was the thing in which the Potter experience could be fictionalized and universalized.

There had been surprisingly little fictional writing about contemporary British politics and certainly very little comedy. Sidney Gilliat's 1959 film *Left, Right and Centre* was a slight piece as was the way with British movies but it was very welcome because of its subject matter. Ian Carmichael plays a television "personality" and panelist who goes north to fight a by-election in the Tory cause. During the campaign he falls in love with his Labour opponent, a university graduate with impeccable working-class credentials played by Patricia Bredin. The centrality of the romance was typical of British cinema at the time but the feel of the constituency and the genuine comedy that developed out of a typical by-election situation, not least those which juxtaposed class styles and pretensions, suggested that this was a subject that young writers should be exploiting. In 1965 Potter came to the subject fresh from his experiences in East Hertfordshire but *Vote, Vote, Vote* did owe something to the stereotypes of the British cinematic traditions, not least the crude opening sequence in which the circumstances that have led to the by-election are explained. A Tory MP breaks his neck whilst riding with the hunt, the other members finding his demise vastly amusing; 'too much brandy' they decide. With that last phrase perhaps we are already moving away from the mood and style of the Launder-Gilliat-Boulting Brothers comedies. The next scene sustains the bitter tone. Nigel Barton and his wife are in their smart London apartment when they hear the news and they both wonder whether they really want to return to fight a by-election in that constituency of 'dreary villages' where he, as the Labour candidate, had been badly beaten in the general election. He accepts that he is under some obligation to return; she indicates that he is perhaps more of a 'charlatan' than that idealistic note would suggest. 'Compromise, compromise, that's the way for you to rise' she taunts.

Vote, Vote, Vote returns to the *Left, Right, Centre* format and style for its play's most famous scene when Nigel Barton turns up at the Civic Dinner and flashes a V-sign at his pompous Tory opponent, an action captured by the photographer and reproduced on all the front pages. This was very much a throwback to the *Lucky Jim* ethos of a decade earlier. It could have come from any of those films in which Ian Carmichael or Dirk Bogarde played a very likeable, attractive, reasonable if rather absent-minded young gent forced temporarily to live amongst provincial yokels. Potter's play is very firmly written from a metropolitan standpoint but unlike the film-studio movies that position has been adopted not so much to poke gentle fun at the world outside the home counties but rather to sustain the bitterness and cynicism. This really is a harsh, unrelenting and unforgiving view of British politics. No real interest whatsoever is shown in the ordinary punters, the voters in the by-election. Everything was being manipulated way above their heads and in any case they are quite hopeless, totally pathetic. They are represented by council estate tenants who 'ought to vote' but never do — for them the election might as well be on the far side of the moon — and by an old man in a nursing home who only wants his leg, a request we are left in no doubt no politician will ever attend to. When faced by the voters Nigel Barton is driven to despair and at one point he is physically sick.

Neither can the candidate find much comfort and camaraderie in the company of his Labour colleagues. Barton is advised 'not to be too clever' and 'to speak slowly as if to malignant children'. This is a pretty hopeless seat for Labour and so what is expected from the candidate is just pure socialism, lots of tub-thumping and no 'lectures on the bank rate'. There is little interest in his talk on the 'present crisis' facing the Labour Government, nobody wants to hear his detailed views on how the economy can be managed. In all these matters both Barton and we, the viewers, are guided by his agent Jack, superbly played by an Enoch Powell look-alike, John Bailey. Jack has seen it all before and certainly he has seen many over-educated, wet-behind-the-ears, London-based parliamentary hopefuls like young Barton come and go. Many of his observations are addressed directly to camera, and this has the effect of underlining the sheer reasonableness of his totally unsentimental cynicism. He effortlessly enlists us to his point of view so that we cannot but question the hopelessness of the whole endeavour. There is no danger at all of any lingering romantic notions of Labour; the Party belongs to the apparatchiks not to the Hampstead trendies. Old Nye was 'a good bloke ... in his way', but that

Suez speech 'lost us a lot of votes, that did!' It has become a party of necessary clichés: the candidate yet again mentions old age pensions and in the audience Jack just crosses himself. If the Tory majority is to be dented what is needed above all is lots of letter-writing to the bereaved, calls on the infirm and aged, plenty of exposure for Quintin Hogg on television and good weather on the day. It's all a question of 'playing by the rules' but Jack knows all very well (and this becomes his last aside to us) that we would 'never vote for Nigel Barton in a million years'. These were hard lessons for the aspiring politician to learn out in the country and Potter's pretty uncompromising cynical note seems harsh even today. In 1965 its tone came as a great surprise given that Labour's return to government after thirteen years in the wilderness was fresh in the memory and that it was not yet generally true that 'the chattering classes' had turned against Harold Wilson. The play's sourness would have been even more appropriate and widely appreciated if shown just two or three years later.

The public scenes were bleak enough but Potter's distinctively personal touch in this play came with the addition of private scenes that offered no respite. Mrs Anne Barton is a beauty but she is there not just to adorn or divert but rather continually to cross-examine her husband about his ideals and motives. In the process candidate and wife trade in brutal home truths and the cutting edge is provided by class. Unlike Nigel she has a middle-class background and so any reference to origins draws blood. 'Your parents', he sneers, 'marked their disillusion with the 1945 election by switching from the *New Statesman* to the *Economist*'. She is rebelling against her family, resents his use of the 'advantage of being born working-class'. She has become the pure idealist, critical of Labour hypocrisy and of his deigning to have anything to do with its shoddy practice by becoming a candidate: 'I thought your Socialism meant more to you than that'. He sees her 'Hampstead socialism' as something that would 'disappear at the first whiff of a navvy's breath', whereas she wants him to be more true to himself, to break with the 'dishonest snobbery' of all other politicians, to give up the clichés, to talk less like a Transport House spokesman and more about his own family background (as documented, she adds in a nice Hampstead touch, in the sociological writings of Jackson and Marsden). Anne's sniping is the best thing in the play and the role was superbly and strongly played by the talented Valerie Gearon. Quite rightly she is allowed her victory. At the Civic Dinner Nigel can take no more of the Tory candidate's rhetoric and with the memory of the pensioner crying for his leg he becomes more and more angry as reference is made to all that 'class waffle'. In his own speech he rejects 'the bromides' he had prepared and finally confronts the fact that his politics could only be explained in terms of his father having been a miner for forty-one years. His father coughed badly but could 'draw an apple in the margin of the paper so good that you could eat it'. That was reality, not the apathy that people took for granted. His listeners soon became restive and beat the tables with their spoons. He explodes and flashes his V-sign. The election is lost but Anne's respect has been won. He is now an honest man, not a time-server and he has earned his right to a safe seat.

The Civic Dinner scene does not really work, either as Lucky Jim type farce or as political comment. Potter does everything he can to stack the odds against the Tory. Captain Luke's dinner jacket is covered with medals and all his references are to be to monarchy, to British greatness and to patriotic causes. His theme is that 'we are all workers now' as evidenced by the fact that his son at Eton 'will do less well than my gardener's son'. As played by Cyril Luckham the Captain does a good job, he touches every base in a truly professional way and fully deserves the rousing chorus of 'He's a Jolly Good Fellow'. In truth nobody in their right mind would vote for his opponent, the rather melancholic and callow outsider waffling on about his father's cough. As politics this just does not come off, but of course Potter's play is not really a piece of advice to Transport House about how it should prepare its candidates for a by-election nor is it a blueprint for how Harold Wilson should solve the balance of payments deficit or stay in office. Certainly the play is a call for Labour to summon up the inspiration that came from its roots, but far more it is about personal integrity and the extent to which we need to understand the basis of our loyalties and come to terms with our own vulnerability. Dennis Potter might well have wanted a new deal for council tenants and a new leg for that pensioner but his play *Vote, Vote, Vote for Nigel Barton* was essentially concerned with the path of discovery a young man had to take so that he could look his wife, his father and himself in the eye. Quite deservedly Nigel Barton had lost his by-election and Potter himself was never again to stand for Parliament. He could turn now to other truths that it was time for Barton to confront.

In *Stand Up, Nigel Barton* we are taken back a few years. Our hero is at Oxford and is just coming to terms with possibilities that his ability has opened up for him. He's in with the smart set of undergraduates; they are all expensive sweaters, posh accents and horn-rimmed spectacles. His particular friend is a judge's daughter. She's quite amused to have a boyfriend with a northern accent, her 'own Andy Capp', but she fancies him and when he acquires his new dinner jacket in preparation for the big Union debate she suggests that he can wear it while they have sex if he wants. She is struck by his earnestness and overwhelming determination to succeed; he is irritated by how her group 'chatter, chatter, chatter' but, she cries, 'that's all I've been trained to do'. At the Union his subject is Class. He knows what he is talking about, the hecklers, of course, wish they did; he wants to be serious, they find that a shame; he dismisses their 'juvenile frivolity', they suspect (wrongly) that he has only hired his dinner jacket (though as he paid for it his thought was of Ramsey MacDonald and class-betrayal). But his speech is a success and it leads directly to an approach from a television producer. 'They've opened the door to let you in', says his girl, but his subsequent attempt to enter that door was painful, for on television he appears to be distancing himself from, and in the process wounding, his parents. The play is about a clever young man, confident of his ability who 'wouldn't mind a job on the telly'. As played by Keith Barron, Nigel Barton, handsome and determined, is obviously well on his way to success.

Those Oxford scenes are only made interesting and only succeed because of Barron's acting, for the other characters are crude stereotypes. Critics were quite rightly to suggest that the playwright had failed to depict a convincing Oxford where in reality we can assume there was an interest in rather more than the externals of young people's personalities. The depiction of television and of journalists was also surprisingly artificial and perfunctory. As had been the case with the constituency in *Vote, Vote, Vote* the reason for these caricatured and underdeveloped scenes was that the author was only really interested in the development of his central character. What is interesting now is that Potter was so confident of Barton (and presumably of Barron too) that that character is allowed to speak directly to camera and so determines our standpoint. This ensures that we view Oxford as outsiders, that we appreciate its privileged artificiality for which, it is explained, we are paying. But it also means that we see the home village that he had recently left as outsiders too. We cut from the Union, with its own rules and conventions, to the club where they play bingo, listen to crude comedians and rile the student who has escaped to a life of luxury as all the while one member croons a sugary ballad. Our intimacy with him leaves us in no doubt that Nigel is too good for Oxford and though they fine him for a drunken escapade we know that he is on his way to success. We can also see that it was imperative that he get away from home. There could be no going back to the village. His mother's point, that his coal- miner father had 'vowed you'd never go down pit', sets up his final bold assertion, his full acceptance of the wind now filling his sails: 'And I bloody well didn't' he boasts. The play can end with a contemporary pop group singing 'We've got to get out of this place, if it's the last thing us ever do'.

This is the basic outline of Nigel Barton's escape from first the village and then Oxford. But Potter fills out the action by concentrating on two crucial relationships. The play begins and ends with Mr Barton Senior, brilliantly played by Jack Woolgar as a constantly coughing, gruff, no-nonsense , hard-headed miner. He is by far the strongest thing in the play and lingers in the mind as much as the most famous miner in English literature, D.H. Lawrence's Mr Morel, to whom he owes not a little. Mr Barton too is not an easy man and certainly needs to sort out one or two of his feelings about his son. He teases him about Oxford and clearly, as his wife maintains, he is jealous of his son's success. When Nigel comes on television he merely wants his son to claim identity with the pit village, he is hurt by his denial and by his description of a father who 'looks at him oddly, like a hawk'. And yet for all his occasional immaturity and anger he is capable of a wise and unsentimental acceptance of the logic inherent in Nigel's development. From the outset he knows that his son is now an Oxford man, he has nothing but contempt for the prying journalist and his anger at his son's television denials soon passes. The play ends with the father and son having at least effected a truce and they go off together for a couple of pints with Mr Barton Senior walking as always in the middle of the road. He is his own man and Nigel Barton has learnt the lesson that this is all we can ever hope to be.

The other relationship that the student Nigel Barton has to come to terms with, the other leftover baggage from the village, was that with his old school. The order for him to 'Stand Up' had come from his schoolteacher and in flashbacks we are taken back to Nigel's childhood and to a classroom ruled over by a gaunt thyroidal disciplinarian given a true Dickensian power by the actress Janet Henfrey. He is her star pupil and is frequently ordered to stand up and show the others how things like reading and reciting should be done. There is little loyalty, though, on her part. She knows that she is exposing him to the contempt of the other children and she is not above reminding him that he, just like the other 'snotty-nosed little kids', comes from a common home. The other kids are quite horrible. All the children, Barton included, are played by adult actors and with this striking innovation Potter neatly makes the points that not only is the child father to the man but that the world of children is as complex, as dangerous and as hurtful as that of adults. In the face of their teasing, their violence, their sheer philistinism, he is driven to prayer, to self-sufficiency and to insult. They are 'bastards' (and one can hear Potter saying this), 'a dirty rotten lot'. We later see the chief school-bully operating as MC in the workingmen's club. Of course Nigel Barton had to get away from this and of course at Oxford he comes to realise that he too had always been walking down the centre of his particular road.

Things are relatively satisfactory at the end of *Stand Up, Nigel Barton*; our hero is kind-of-mates with his dad and presumably is now off for a successful career in television and marriage to the judge's daughter. We can only have confidence in this character, especially as brought to life by Keith Barron. There is a contrast, though, between the relatively satisfactory outcome (after all, one could envisage alternative endings with the parents rejecting him or with his having a nervous breakdown) and the disturbing tone of the play. The action throughout comes to us in a rapid succession of short scenes in all of which there is tension and struggle; the contrasts are always made sharply and so we are never allowed to settle or to feel comfortable. Everybody is getting at Nigel Barton in one way or another, he is given little respite and so it is no wonder that he needs us to confide in. The story shows us a resilient and accomplished young man succeeding and we can believe in that; such careers are not unusual at any time and were particularly common in the 1950s and 1960s. But in this version of a talent flourishing the bitterness of some of the personal experience lingers on and inevitably one wonders whether even someone as apparently confident as Nigel Barton will totally obliterate the memories. At the Union debate he refers to his having had to negotiate 'the minefield of class'. We have been given examples of that minefield but we never doubt that he will cope. More serious is the minefield of personal feelings and there the detonations seem altogether of a different order. A child who is driven to private prayer out of fear of a teacher's wrath or a class bully is experiencing something a little deeper than being teased about his accent. Every adolescent moves away from his or her parents, and often there is reflection at the first lie, the first suppressed information and the first rearrangement of loyalty, but rarely is there such a dramatic renunciation as in this play. Barton sits with his parents in their own home and they all watch his betrayal of them on national television. The comic and stereotypical writing for the mother ('you can eat off the floor') does not disguise the almost Biblical dimensions of this denial. One can almost hear the cock crowing.

Even on its first showing in 1965 there must have been many viewers who would have realised that Barton had been put through an experience very similar to that undergone by the author himself and referred to, of course, in his earlier autobiographical writings. Now with hindsight we can see how much of Barton's story was shaped by Potter's memories. Later we would learn more about his unhappiness at school and about his preoccupations with various kinds of guilt. In particular, of course, the passing of time would reveal that, however much Keith Barron's version of Barton had reflected elements of the real-life Potter, the author was to follow a career in which he became more concerned with the disturbing, troublesome aspects of *Stand Up* rather than one which followed on from his character's public strengths in the play. That duality, that contrast between Barron/Barton's confidence and style and the unpleasant nature of his experiences and relationships is there in the play and might raise questions in the minds of some first-time viewers about the rather too easy and sudden ending. Inevitably those of us familiar with Potter's later career will see this play as the one in which the author confronted the duality in his own life. For some time he had known, and time would confirm, that illness would prevent him from being the public man Keith Barron's acting had suggested. It was with the internal wounds of persecution and guilt that the writer would now be increasingly concerned.

Criticisms of *Stand Up* have always concentrated on the exaggerated nature of its class contrasts. T.C. Worsley thought its concept of Oxford 'some ten to fifteen years out of touch with the subject' and lacking the vitality and novelty value of Emlyn Williams' play *The Corn is Green* which had dealt with a similar subject and which had been written in 1938. Writing in 1965 D.A.N. Jones took the point that Potter himself had directly experienced 'the dramatic clash of two revered (and obsolescent) elites, Oxford students and coalminers' but quite rightly stressed that 'the wounding alienation of the schoolboy exists at many levels—even for a skilled craftsman's son in the A stream of a comprehensive'. The clear implication here is that Potter had made too much of Barton's experiences, that there had been excessive special-pleading, an altogether too obvious attempt to enlist our pity. Time and time again Potter's critics were to fault him for class caricature and self-pity in ways that revealed that their own preoccupation with sociological generalities had prevented them from accepting the invitation to consider the implications of personal hurt that the playwright had offered. There are indeed instances in which it is precisely the political arrogance or correctness (to use the new vocabulary of the nineties) of the critic or scholar which helps us appreciate the highly individual approach that Potter was now attempting to define. Writing from the perspective of 1989, the literary scholar Alan Sinfield characterised *Stand Up* as being 'shot through with guilt and self-satisfaction' and argued that the representation of working people had been arranged solely 'to alleviate the guilt of the class-mobile' with the consequence that 'the play re-enacts the exploitation that it appears to criticize'. The slick dismissiveness of that so-neat academic term "the class-mobile" reveals a critical mentality more concerned with confirming well-established political reference-points than attempting to empathise with personal crises.

Potter's development as a television dramatist was now to take him well away from his initial *Nigel Barton* format, but before we follow that development it is interesting to note at this point that five years and some eight plays later he was to write a play that is generally regarded as completing an autobiographical trilogy. Clearly *Lay Down Your Arms* was inspired by Potter's experience of National Service in the 1950s which he had spent as a Russian-language clerk in the War Office. As with the two Nigel Barton plays the playwright is dramatizing scenes from his own career but now his *alter ego* has been renamed. And quite rightly so, for here the hero reacts to the challenge of class in significantly different ways, ways which tell us more about the development of Potter than the play's ostensible subject. This was Potter's Suez play and he uses his hero's vantage point as a humble War Office clerk savagely to condemn the class and racial prejudices of a hopelessly snobbish and effete public school élite who are seen to be determining government policy at this time of crisis and national humiliation. This was a big, ambitious subject and both author and director (Christopher Morahan) employed a number of striking techniques in order to establish both the significance of the issue and the depth of their feelings. We are being asked to consider the Empire and the way it was run, and newsreel footage, flashbacks, London location shots and a heavily emphasised title-song are all used portentously. Meanwhile in one crowded room (and the claustrophobia is emphasised by the contrast between location and studio shooting) the clerk observes and is joshed by a group of upper-class twits. Much of this is badly overdone, overblown and cliché-ridden and even in 1970 must have been ineffective as a critique, both of what had happened in the Suez crises and of British politics. It is hardly surprising that Potter's play about 1956 has not lingered in the nation's cultural memory in the same way as the Barton plays about a slightly later era have done. For those viewers, however, who were more interested in the author's general development than in his precise politics *Lay Down Your Arms* was fascinating at a very different level.

The protagonist, the War Office clerk who is called Hawk, is altogether a different type from the Nigel Barton of Keith Barron. As played by Nikolas Simmonds he is good-looking and obviously intelligent but in general his physique is that of an athlete and perhaps someone who trains and works out alone. Hawk has none of Barton's refinement, none of his social graces and nothing of that very English sense of ease which in his case had suggested that every obstacle would eventually be overcome. Barton's style would have seen him through but Hawk is altogether a more awkward customer. He is shaped more in the American, and more specifically the Marlon Brando, mould for he is a loner, a more silent, moody and charmless type. At the outset we see his anger, as in his pronounced northern working-class accent he tells some American tourist 'to get stuffed'. Potter had clearly gone for a bleaker and more alien intruder from the class underworld so as to highlight the affectation of the Whitehall élite but in so doing he was opening up other possibilities. Of course Hawk is alienated by the War Office lulus but what is really fascinating about his situation is the extent to which he is alienated from everybody else as well. In effect he is telling everyone to get stuffed. In several scenes he visits his parents in their northern working-class home and here too Potter has learnt his lesson for now there is no Jack Woolgar to steal the show. Rather Dad is a fairly unremarkable and irritating Yorkshire bore, one of those smart-alec and tedious miners who go on and on about how they were sold out by their leader in 1926 and who now vote Tory. For Hawk there is no companionship at home and neither is there amongst the more humble folk in London; the corporal with whom he works and has a lunchtime drink talks entirely in clichés and catch-phrases. After 'one for the road' with his 'old mate', it's 'noses back to the grindstone'. Our hero is alienated from something more than a public-school-run Empire and in truth the jibes that come from his class enemies about his not having a girl-friend cut more deeply than their snobbish and reactionary value judgments. He is almost embarrassed into spending his last thirty bob on losing his virginity with a Soho tart, and then he breaks down and cries as he lies about his love life to parents anxious about his obvious loneliness. Anne Shelton belts out the title song as if she is standing in front of the whole British army but in requesting the laying down of arms and a surrendering to her she is obviously addressing the needs of an individual soldier boy.

Hawk is an unhappy young man and with him we never feel as we did with Nigel Barton that success both in politics and in love were bound to come once he had sorted out a few hang-ups. Hawk will always remain dissatisfied and ill at ease but at least as the play progresses we begin to understand the activities that will offer him most relief and satisfaction. He is of course an intellectual and therefore quite out of place in either Yorkshire or Whitehall. He has learnt the beauty of the Russian language and therein, to the bewilderment of his colleagues, he finds insight into the nature of his soul. In his work he comes across a letter from a Russian tank officer to the officer's coalminer father and the 'beauty' of that teaches him that 'sometimes you don't know how you feel until someone has written it down for you'. What is most interesting about Hawk is not his politics but the development of his imagination. His loneliness and his sheer frustration drive him to fantasise Billy Liar style; he tells others of girl-friends who are either Russian ballerinas or actresses at the Old Vic and in the play's most important and memorable scene he convinces a whole bar full of pub bores that he is is none other than Lev Yashin, the legendary goalkeeper of Moscow Dynamo who are at that moment in London to play a match. It is hardly surprising that later in the play two friends refuse to believe him when he explains how he has access to top secret files; they think he is 'just being Yashin again'. He steals a file to prove his point but of course his friends fail to keep the appointment in the park; inevitably they had not taken him seriously. In disgust Hawk throws the file to the ducks who quack appreciatively. End of play; once again Anne Shelton sings her orders but whose arms have been laid down? Britain has been humiliated but doubtless Whitehall will go on being a playground for grown up public schoolboys. Clearly Potter and his director want us to be indignant about that. But do we really care? Does Hawk care? Surely he has fed secrets to the ducks not as the first act of a new career in political dissent but rather because he is off to the provinces to become a writer, to create his Lev Yashins on paper. It is to the arms of his muse that he has surrendered. Potter had wanted to condemn an Empire and its upper-class rulers but what he had really done is to explain how one young man had come to realise how infinitely more satisfying it is to devise one's own worlds than to change the one ordered by other people.

Hawk would never be an easy citizen in the way that was within Nigel Barton's capacity but long before his creation Dennis Potter had already given notice that his most distinctive and memorable plays would not be about "class-mobiles" overcoming external obstacles and personal hurt but about protagonists unable to cope with the insensibility of society. The socially accomplished Nigel Barton had really been stung by other people's malevolent arrogance and desire to wound and now Potter began to investigate how people who had no real self-defence or who were in some way greatly disadvantaged were taunted and abused by the socially secure and confident. He would be suggesting that a degree of violence was a natural outcome of such social misunderstanding and cruelty and that ultimately the victims would be crushed. Potter, it seemed, was not going to be an easy playwright for increasingly he wanted his audiences to confront the sheer ugliness of how the disadvantaged were made to suffer social hypocrisy. Now forced by circumstances to make his living as a television playwright Potter moved sharply away from that high political and metropolitan world of the Macmillan-Wilson era in which Nigel Barton had seemed destined to make his mark and suddenly he was rummaging around for victims in anonymous and undistinguished localities very far indeed from the sixties' glamour that the media so wanted to celebrate. It did not take him long to identify the elements of what was to be Potterland. Quite remarkably *Where The Buffalo Roam*, first broadcast in 1966, the year in which Harold Wilson renewed his electoral mandate, not only introduces us to what were to develop into the playwright's major preoccupations but also to an urban bleakness that was to become a far more generally discussed and analysed phenomenon in the decades of de-industrialisation that lay several years ahead.

It is a very simple play. Willy (and that very name establishes one theme immediately) is a young Swansea lad who lives with his widowed mother and his grandfather. In his time he has been a bed-wetter and a stutterer and he still has pronounced learning difficulties, not least his inability to read. His mother is too soft, totally blind as to the nature of his problems, whilst his grandfather knows that Willy is a bad'un, very much the son of a father who had been a violent womaniser, and in their continual bickering he frequently warns that 'behind bars ... is where he'll end up'. There is no respite at school where a teacher humiliates him in front of the class and dismisses him as 'stupid' as yet again he reveals his difficulty with reading. Willy needs an alternative to the unpleasantness of home and the hell of school and he finds it in the cinema and in particular in Western movies. His life has become a fantasy focused on Abilene and Laredo, and those who antagonise him or who fail to understand him are merely instructed to call him "Shane". The wounding humiliations continue on all fronts and so Willy resorts to the methods of his fictional heroes; he actually shoots his family, his grandfather's pigeons and a policeman. There can only be one ending. He is pursued across roof-tops by armed police and a Hollywood-type shoot-out ends with Willy being shot and then plunging to his death crying not 'top of the world, Ma' but 'Geronimo' and 'Daddy'.

To watch *Where The Buffalo Roam* twenty-five years after it was first broadcast is to be struck by its prescience. Here is a fundamental text for that great debate that developed in the 1980s about the connection between popular culture and violence and which focused specifically on "massacres" such as that at Hungerford and their possible inspiration in Sylvester Stallone's *Rambo* movies. For almost a century civic leaders and social observers had speculated about the capacity of film to promote juvenile anger and crime but in the post-industrial era the powerful mix of new weaponry, urban blight and the skilful commercial projection of images of sex and sanctioned rebellion seemed to be leading to unprecedented horrors demanding a more sophisticated analysis. Potter's play is certainly highly relevant to any sociologist or psychologist working to make that analysis, not least in the way in which the language neatly contrasts the possibilities allowed by fantasy and denied by the reality: 'Riding the Range, that's a good job' — 'Not in Swansea it's not'. The final shoot-out is, of course, pure Cagney but those factory roofs, the cold store and the crane catch something of the drabness and sheer desolate meaninglessness of so much urban space in a way that is very unusual in a

British film. This is not to say that the play is uniformly effective. It is now a very dated television play with that uneasy mix of studio and location shooting. Hywel Bennett is very good, as he was always to be, at playing not quite grown up young men and at sustaining the otherwise never explicit sexual allegory suggested by his character's name. But he is not given good support in the domestic scenes for Megs Jenkins is too refined to be his mother and the wife of her much maligned dead husband, and Aubrey Richards is far too young to convey the full sense of a grandfather's indignation. The home is vital in this play, that is where the damage is done, and yet the acting is not quite precise enough to clinch the point. Potter's message, though, is straightforward enough; the damage done in the past by a violent father prevents the remaining members of what is obviously an incomplete family from focusing on the immediate needs of a son cruelly beaten by his father and now very obviously needing precisely a father's love and understanding to guide him through to adult relationships.

One would assume that normally there would be agencies to help families such as Willy's but in this respect Potter adds what we can now see to be a distinctive touch to the story. Again the teacher is a villain, concerned only to ridicule publicly the disadvantaged pupil, but to the classroom scenes Potter adds another in which the teacher meets the probation officer who is just beginning to unravel the family circumstances that may have created Willy's reading problems. As they discuss the schoolboy's cowboy fantasies so these two professional middle-aged men, both graduates, both (we can safely conclude) *Guardian*-reading liberals, discover that they are both Western enthusiasts themselves. The probation officer has genuine understanding and in this conversation he manages to find the humanity in the schoolteacher for as they talk about the films so the classroom authoritarianism of the latter falls away. These are not bad men but of course that is not the sole point that Potter is making. Their sociological analysis of the Western genre, their regretting the rise of the psychological Western, their nostalgia for cinema and their joking references to each other as "pardners" are all very well but the middle-class can effortlessly live with their day-dreams and affectations. But what can they do to rescue those individuals who do not have the intellectual and emotional resources to reconcile attractive fictions with social imperatives? In *Where The Buffalo Roam* Potter had clearly opted to follow up the kind of individual hurt that had been only one element in the maturing of Nigel Barton. His subject now was the total vulnerability of the young, even within the very circumstances where they should be at their safest, but although the family has been brought more sharply into focus society itself is not allowed off the hook. Perhaps the most wounding thing of all is just how easy things are for those people who seem to know the rules.

The intervening years have made the story of Willy much more plausible than it must have seemed in 1966 but of course his protest is extreme and his demise sensational and to that extent the play strikes one as having been written too deliberately as a shocker. Things are far more of a piece in Potter's 1968 play *A Beast With Two Backs*. Here the elements cohere and the cruelty, the lies and the tragedies grow out of a set of characters and a specific society that we get to know in the round. Every incident here, even those that shock, seems all too plausible and in a way their very inevitability greatly deepens the several tragedies that bring the action to an end. The maturing dramatist has learnt the importance of sharply defining character and mood and of integrating violence into the natural rhythms of the society depicted. Again the theme is that violence which is aimed at innocent and defenceless victims by a largely unthinking range of individuals and groups, none of whom had ever realized the way that their quite normal feelings and prejudices only barely constrained strong and malicious passions which were all too likely to spill out at times of excitement and crisis. At the play's end a performing bear is stoned to death by a crowd which thinks it guilty of having killed a village girl. Meanwhile the local preacher whose sermon had at first unwittingly and then deliberately directed the crowd towards the bear commits suicide in the belief that it was his retarded son Rufus who had attacked the girl and in so doing almost killed her (indeed to protect his son it was he who had eventually delivered the *coup de grace*). As the angry crowd return to the village they pass the fleeing Rufus, a figure they have taunted for years; that crowd of course includes Micky Teague, the man we have actually seen using a heavy stone to strike down the girl who was his mistress and who had just revealed that she was pregnant. All this amounts to a sensational enough tale but not for one moment do we doubt its veracity; the text, the direction and the acting all see to that.

As Philip Purser has stressed, this was the first play that Potter had set entirely in his native Forest of Dean and location filming ensured that the landscape was used to full effect. Purser suggests that the story of the performing bear was one that Potter had heard in his childhood and certainly the late Victorian period setting seems absolutely right for the crowd psychology that he needs to develop. Quite apart from the authentic period detail the production sustains an ever deeper and fuller sense of the past because scenes are set in an old church and amidst ancient ruins. History presses down on the action and the whole story takes on the feel of a much retold classic that is part of our heritage; this could almost be Boccaccio. The whole point of this heavy emphasis on established community is that every bit of this isolated and introverted society is riddled with unpleasantness, hypocrisy and duplicity. Everybody, whatever their class or section, is guilty of something and yet there is a conspiracy to ensure that life continues normally without any of these moral shortcomings being confronted. In the pub the miners cruelly taunt the retarded Rufus drawing specific attention to his speech difficulty and his sexual backwardness. All of this is justified of course because, as with the heavy drinking, the blaspheming and sexual innuendo, the miners 'need a bit of fun before going back to the pit on Monday'. Rufus is dragged from the pub and beaten by his father Ebenezer, a hell-fire preacher who battles every week to cure his congregation of miners and their families of their heavy drinking and sexual promiscuity. He is at his wits end with Rufus, no longer quite able to restrain a son who has 'the body not the soul of a man', and at night the youth has to be tied to his bed and locked in his room. We are left to ponder the love, the guilt, the frustration and the anger that has characterized this household over the years. Meanwhile we have seen one miner, Micky Teague, brutally striking down Rebecca who had pleaded with him to leave his wife and acknowledge that he was the father of the child she was carrying. Early on Teague tells Rebecca that he feels 'like a snake' when he sees his wife, yet later his wife is quite prepared to provide him with an alibi when the police call: better by far to have a wage-earning husband even if he has had to murder his mistress. For his part the police inspector suspects that even if Teague was Rebecca's lover he was just one amongst many. If there is evil afoot in this village then clearly there will be many accomplices. Even the young children have already imbued the general immorality of the place for it is they who first invent the lies that arouse suspicions about the itinerant Italian Joe and his performing bear.

A whole community, then, stands condemned and clearly the indictment has been prepared by a writer who knows of what he speaks. In a small isolated English mining village other observers would choose to pick on exploitation, solidarity or religious devotion but Potter knows that here precisely is where he will find the private and public cruelty and intolerance to sustain his tale. He is quite prepared to be open about it although there is more than a suggestion that he jokes about the identification of the locale as if to soften the critique. The play opens with Joe talking to his bear and pointing down to the Forest of Dean village which he dreads. 'Mama Mia, this is not easy', he complains, with much the same tone that Willy Loman uses for New England. The irony is sustained, the kids shout at him as he takes a pee in the woods; 'I don't like this place', he says as he crosses himself. In the centre of the village this Italian entertainer announces his act. 'You talk funny', comments a local girl; 'are you from Gloucester?'. All the signposts are very clear, although as the tragedies unfold the power of this particular story leads one to speculate about those countless examples in history when a local crime, especially if it was sexually motivated, was immediately attributed to a visitor, to an outsider or to anyone who was different. Blacks and Jews, of course, were often victimized in these circumstances.

In Potter's story the innocent Italian and his bear are made to suffer as the miners give vent to their immediate anger and to their more long-term prejudices, but that, as the title of the play has made clear, is not the only reason why the author has introduced a bear into the Forest of Dean. The pivotal moment in the play comes when Ebenezer in his pulpit confronts a congregation that is considerably larger than usual, for the murder has driven many back to church for the first time since Christmas. Ebenezer knows that they are there because 'there's wickedness in the woods, Satan is stalking our streets'. They have all 'smelt wickedness in the vile maggotty streets'. He slips into his full Old Testament prophet mode and quotes Job as he switches his argument to tell them that there is also wickedness in all their hearts. He is, of course, trying to tell them that they are not much better than his son Rufus whom he assumes to be the criminal but, as he argues that man is a beast and that it is 'the beast within' and the 'Beast of Baal' that has to be confronted and driven out, his audience begins to draw their own conclusions. His 'Come out, come out now bloody beast' leads on to 'Hunt it down' and so the tragic denouement is set under way. At first old Ebenezer (as played by Dennis Carey) had seemed a very much overdone parody of a preacher but he comes into his own in this magnificent sermon. The director has cheated slightly for this truly Nonconformist type is given a splendid Anglican church to lend authority to his words. Ebenezer has already confessed that there is a 'temper in me like old Adam', and of course it is the old Adam in every man that he is condemning in his tirade. Sex is the evil that runs right through the Forest of Dean community. The bear, whose only appetite we ever see is for honey, is nature at its most innocent and splendid; she remains the only admirable character in the play. As she dies after her very Biblical stoning in the quarry Joe calls her name, 'Gina', and mourns her as a friend. Rufus has appetites he does not understand whilst too many villagers might understand but have no control. It is what Rebecca, Micky Teague and who knows how many others have been doing illicitly in the woods that leads directly to tragedy.

A Beast With Two Backs was a highly accomplished piece of television and a very good example of how much this medium had achieved in Britain during the 1960s. There were still many who bemoaned the failure of Britain to develop its own film culture, its own national cinema, not realising that this was now precisely the role that television drama was fulfilling. A small group of writers, directors and producers had put televised drama at the centre of both cultural debate and popular interest in a way that the film studios had rarely accomplished. Already there was widespread recognition of Dennis Potter's important contribution to this very exciting cultural breakthrough. As early as 1967 the respected and influential critic T.C. Worsley was referring to Potter as 'one of the few writers on either channel to whose plays I turn with high expectations'. What he liked most about the writer was that his stories had obviously been 'conceived ... in vividly televisual terms' and so there was usually in his broadcast work 'a skilful exploitation of all resources of the medium', with every advantage being 'taken of the technical devices' and of 'that freedom of movement in both time and place' which he took to be television's 'particular virtue'. In other words Potter was now recognised as a highly professional writer for television and it was his proficiency and dependability in that respect which allowed him not only to find regular outlets for his individual plays but also to graduate to the writing of a highly original six-part version of the Casanova story, an exercise which suggested that he could always supplement his income by writing television adaptations and mini-series. Worsley also noted Potter's ability to immediately alight on 'themes which the times throw up at him' so that his plays were always of 'lively contemporary interest'. It was *Vote, Vote, Vote* , a play about a by-election first broadcast between two general elections ending thirteen years of Tory rule, which had opened Potter's eyes to the value of topicality, and it was a lesson from which he continued to draw inspiration. Plays such as *Message for Posterity* (a great statesman has his portrait painted) and *Traitor* (about an English defector in Moscow) as well as the belated Suez play, *Lay Down Your Arms*, all fed off widespread popular debates.

To those in the business of broadcasting and reviewing it was certainly Potter's sheer professionalism that was most evident. But for that great television audience, most of whom put their sets on at six and then left them on for the evening without ever reading the credits, the name of this particular playwright was becoming notorious for rather different reasons. There was now competition between the channels and so already, albeit in small and rather innocent ways compared to what was to follow in the 1980s, the companies were beginning to hype their forthcoming attractions. But with Potter it was more than hype, it was just plain controversy. With almost every play there was a row, sometimes before transmission and always afterwards. His first ever play had brought threats of a lawsuit and then the BBC had delayed *Vote,*

Vote, Vote and demanded script changes. And so it went on. In his 1970 play, *Angels Are So Few*, a loveless married couple are seen watching a television play about the making of a blue movie. Inevitably, in a phrase that was beginning to be applied to every Potter film, it was referred to as 'the most controversial offering of the year'. A year later Mrs Whitehouse condemned one of the *Casanova* plays for its 'lewdness and gross indecency'. The playwright defended his work and told his critic to 'hold her tongue'. Soon there was a well-established routine attending the screening of every Potter play and although the possible obstacles and then the objections and complaints must have sometimes angered the writer, as well as possibly temporarily threatening his livelihood, one also suspects that all this attention was not entirely displeasing to him or his producers. Every author wants to be noticed, and what could be more satisfying with a bland medium like television than for there to be guaranteed and widespread anticipation and subsequent debate? One senses that at least in part Potter had come to enjoy the licence he had in effect been given to participate in the process whereby television became more explicit about sex and a whole range of other cultural subjects which had previously been taboo. He certainly enjoyed being the main brunt of the suburban puritan backlash. On the one hand the television producers had half- opened a door which Potter was all prepared to leap through, while on the other the knee-jerk protesters ensured that the notoriety which he had so easily accomplished a decade earlier in the era of anger was now sustained in very different circumstances. To one extent the television companies and Mrs Whitehouse conspired to create a situation in which Dennis Potter was invited to shock.

Professional and controversial, Potter's place in the culture had been quickly defined and guaranteed. There were only a few people, however, who knew the full circumstances that had contributed to the making of this career forged in television and of the price the author himself had paid. A promising and indeed hitherto successful young man had seemed destined for a career at the very hub of that nexus of radical politics, journalistic flair and television irreverence that was transforming the intellectual life of London in the early 1960s. Suddenly this ambitious and gregarious young man had been struck down by an extremely painful, debilitating and unsightly illness which was almost certainly occasioned in part by a breakdown of some sort. That man, still only thirty, had withdrawn from London to the total anonymity of the countryside and there in circumstances of the utmost physical humiliation and pain he had sustained and redirected his creative energies. Certain preoccupations remained. He was still a very political animal; Potter was always to insist on this point. He was never to lose his very 1950s sense that for reasons that are all too obvious certain people have things easy. His attention had shifted, though, away from a preoccupation with privilege and hypocrisy and had become far more concentrated on impediment and the need for solace. Undoubtedly it was the dramatic and sudden transition, both in terms of his condition and his location, which went into the creation of what was becoming quintessential Potter. Nigel Barton was all too aware of memories from home that could never be shaken off but now Potter had returned to within a few miles of his old home. What was to be unique about his literary world was the way in which the fashionable concerns of the post 1960s era — class, the media, popular culture, sex and nostalgia — were used by him to explore problems of cruelty, illness, domestic anguish and religious belief which were in general unfashionable but which now came readily to Potter's mind as he recalled his own childhood and contemplated his own condition. As the decades went by it became increasingly clear that much of British politics and culture were dominated by grammar school and university trained writers for whom the Welfare State, the BBC and Hollywood had defined a comfortable universe whose norms were sacrosanct. Potter had been part of that whole cultural phenomenon but events and illness had forced him to consider the fate of casualties and how they fare at the hands of family, friends and of the God whom they had been taught to respect. Everything about the cultural revolution of the 1960s was aimed at defining and projecting comfortable and fashionable images. More than ever before a whole range of social groups were conditioned to develop lifestyles in which items such as clothing, household goods and furnishings, music, accents and vocabulary would be carefully selected from a variety of established cultures whether they be proletarian, continental, newly designed or

American. Television played a key role in this whole process, with television drama in particular helping to sustain very clear notions of urban culture both past and present. The essence of Potter emerged out of his unique understanding of the whole interplay between the new cultural energies and the possibilities of a powerful medium that had both a life and values of its own. Necessarily things were tending to a new consensus but meantime he had unfashionable things to tell his audiences. All too often he was discussed as if he were a prophet of the new permissive sexual revolution, but rather he was more like his character Ebenezer, a prophet that knows that for himself, as perhaps for many other people who did not care to admit it, the greatest difficulty in life was not grabbing hold of what was new but rather shaking off aspects of the past. Through television Potter would ask questions which so many other groups both old and new, left and right, had decided were best left unconsidered. His own past and his own new circumstances allowed him to provide the underside of a new culture which was rapidly becoming as smug and confident as the one which it set out to replace.

Potterland

For Dennis Potter the 1970s were years of illness and isolation. Later he was to recall moments when he was 'unable to move much else besides my left arm and maybe my penis'. Inevitably television loomed large in such an existence; for the suffering patient it could never be the bland source of background conversation and jingles it was for other people with busy routines to fulfil. Potter the viewer could develop into the arch critic all too aware of the hours of cliché and pap, whereas Potter the professional writer, all too grateful for a livelihood, could master the art of television drama in all its various forms. What was to be increasingly recognised as his distinctive genre of writing, what we may justifiably term "Potterland", clearly developed out of this tension. Fired by his own dissatisfaction and his need to obtain his own sense of ambition and worth he deliberately set out to create plays that would disturb the overwhelming tendency of the small screen to present a trite, unrelievedly naturalistic world. In his 1984 Preface to *Waiting for the Boat* he succinctly and eloquently summed up that very easy and small world of television and suggested that what had happened in Britain was that the cosy and smug atmosphere of the commercial breaks had suffused the actual programmes, not least those that dealt in fictions. Quite simply Potter had decided to become a television playwright who deliberately set out 'to disorientate the viewer'. He would do that first in terms of subject matter and then increasingly in terms of production techniques.

To argue that the very singularity, not to say extremity, of Potter's physical position made him all too aware of the nature of television is an obvious point. The question of the extent to which

Potterland was the direct product of the privation and suffering arising out of the author's particularly debilitating, painful, humiliating and utterly personal illness is a more complex matter, although one that needs to be discussed only briefly. As always Potter himself has half-opened the door of conjecture before infuriatingly, but understandably, slamming it. In that 1984 Preface, although 'half afraid', he more or less concedes that an outbreak of sheer disgust that affects the central character Jack in his 1972 *Follow the Yellow Brick Road* 'represented' to a degree what he 'felt at that time about the cold or faithless world and its suffocating materiality', or his 'cold and faithless self'. The admission was carefully swaddled in qualifications and distancing. Obviously, argues Potter, a man as disturbed as the Jack of the scene in question would never be 'capable of one modicum of the detachment, let alone the discipline, needed to write such a scene' and then he tags on the suggestion that surely the more an author's writing becomes merely a 'form of personal therapy' the less good it becomes. The play itself must always be the focus of attention. The later Potter of the 1980s was to become much more of a public figure. Occasional remission and a confidence engendered by artistic success enabled him to grant interviews during which clues could be released about the true nature of his illness, an illness described by Adam Mars-Jones as being 'particularly malevolent'. Of course, Potter told Mars-Jones, 'anyone who has an illness more than fleetingly must form a relationship with it' and possibly even develop 'affinities with it'. For *The Observer* he described his affliction as his 'strange shadowy ally'.

We must certainly note, then, that combination of influences that produced a Potterland in the 1970s and which allowed his work to achieve a much-acclaimed fruition. A creative writer, almost totally committed to writing television drama, and drama that was designed to be good and powerful to the extent that it challenged and disturbed both critics and a mass audience, was on the whole largely confined to his own home by psoriatic arthropathy, an illness that guaranteed pain, deformity, discomfort and a degree both of identification with and alienation from a body that seemed to have taken on a horrifying will of its own. Surely it is not too glib to suggest that although much of the old political and social anger of the 1950s and 1960s had evaporated, Potter was uniquely placed both to sustain his own individual share of what had been his generation's anger and to widen and deepen it by continually searching for that point in which the exploitative and hypocritical aspects of society could interact with personal weakness and frailty and with the various emotional comforts and palliatives conventionally on offer. He had been led to that nexus by the dramatic circumstances that had affected him in the mid-1960s. He had been given his subject and now in the years that followed that alliance between his belief in the power and cultural centrality of television and the intense and immediate sense of his own circumstances became the basis of his search for subject matter in which variations on that fundamental nexus could be developed. Undoubtedly Potter wanted to shock, wanted to be noticed, and that too became part of the alliance, but the impetus towards disorientation and sensation in his work never seemed merely mischievous or gratuitous because, although he was never writing mere autobiography, he was at the very least all too aware from his own experiences of how dramatic and cruel real life could be. By the same token the degree to which the vital action of a play grew out of personal crisis often meant that the overall form of the play seemed less satisfactory and less memorable than the particular moments when individual characters experienced before our very eyes the full horrors of their own particular dilemma. Clearly the writer had preoccupations, themes suggested by his past, by his present circumstances and by what might have been. He was working those themes and all the while broadening the possibilities of television drama.

The *Nigel Barton* plays had given Potter a fleeting fame in the 1960s at a time when it was generally expected that young men would be angry. Thereafter his steady output reminded critics and discerning viewers that, like many other early rebels, he was still essentially looking for a post-sixties niche. Perhaps some of them had noted that *A Beast With Two Backs* had been a really accomplished piece of work but it was to be his 1969 play *Son of Man* which first indicated the extent to which Potter was going to be an awkward customer, an irritant in the national culture of television, a writer working against the grain, picking at sores and probing scars that suburban society had been trained to forget. This was the play that opens the central period of his career, the period that was to produce his most memorable and satisfying work. In the last years of the sixties Potter had now chosen to write a play about Jesus. The decade, of course, had been one of the most secular on record. Occasionally in the 1950s the nation had agonised about whether God had a role in South Africa, whether he lived in a Heaven above or was merely a metaphor, but thereafter suburban families and the young had lived in a world free of external constraint or judgement. By 1969 Christianity was somewhat out of fashion and so it was from a position of considerable detachment that most viewers turned to *Son of Man*. The general reaction, as Philip Purser noted, was not extreme and that was because most people, whether believers or no, interpreted the play very much in terms of its central assertion and argument that the crucifixion and the subsequent salvation of mankind were only valid if the Son of God had really become the Son of Man. The assumption was that Potter had merely made the rather neat, but perhaps obvious and not altogether surprising point given man's view of his own importance in the 1960s, that Christ had been a real and therefore ordinary person capable of anger, irritation, doubt and fear. Much of that, of course, is actually in the Gospels as anyone who had been brought up like the playwright in a Bible-based Nonconformist sect would know. What surprise there was in that initial showing was created by the peasant stockiness, earthiness, plainness and sheer disgruntlement of the actor Colin Blakeley. The casting had seemed altogether more remarkable than the story itself. Certainly the impact of the play was lessened just as the sheer ordinariness of Blakeley himself was enhanced by the very obvious studio setting. There was nothing here of Hollywood's exotic and garish Calvaries nor of the memorable magic of Pier Paolo Pasolini's *The Gospel According to St Matthew* of 1964 in which a Marxist Christ had walked through a recognisable Italy.

More than with any other Potter play this is a text that needs to be revisited. One needs, further, to imagine the text being read from the start by the author. Jesus has been in the wilderness for forty days and now a voice only he can hear tells him that his time has come. We are told in the instructions that this Jesus is croaking or gabbling his own words but perhaps the actor or reader should be told to aim for a whine: 'Speak! Please, my father. Speak to me.

'Speak to me-e!'. This is the essential tone of the play and one wishes that it had been done first as a radio play with the emphasis very fully on this central relationship between a highly fearful, apprehensive Jesus and the voice he has to respond to but without ever being fully confident that the exact nature of his sacrifice is comprehended: 'Is it — TIME! Is it — me? Me?'. This is the Jesus whom a disciple will see 'topple into his own spew' as he pleads with his Father to let him 'be just a man', a crucified Christ who will all too understandably cry out 'Why have you forsaken me?' and who in the most remarkable passage of the play speaks to a 'Dada' who can be seen and comprehended in 'love' in 'the thrust and fall and thigh and odour', 'in the curling of a leaf on the face of man' as well as 'in the dung and the slime puss piss snail snake scab' and 'in the scream the torment the fever of the sick'.

Potter had introduced God back into the agenda of television drama but this was not the God of the suburbs of those refined English aesthetes who confined him to a world of stained-glass and lovely music. This was a God of the sects, of followers who had been brought up to talk to him as if he were a member of the family: a God with whom contact was not confined to moments of philosophical or aesthetic reflection or indeed to well-rehearsed exercises of liturgy or rhetoric but rather one who approached at precisely those times when one was aware of one's shortcomings and failures. This God could infuriate both by being elusive when needed most but also by being all too immediate when one felt exposed and vulnerable. In depicting a Jesus battling to ensure his own humanity Potter had really written a play in which he either reminded or informed us of the extent to which any individual believer can have a relationship with a God who is at one moment a 'Dada' and at the next has disappeared or become ambiguous, and that the leap into an experience of God or a cry unto his name is more likely to come from pain than from recollections in tranquility. This is a play about basic bedrock belief, and of course its inevitable companion, doubt, a play about a troubled man's need for a 'Dada' every bit as much as one about the Son of God needing to be a man. In 1969 there were not many people ready to contemplate what was involved in a personal God, and perhaps it was to take the later more confident and more confessional voice of Potter himself to explain how much of himself there was in this play and what prayer can really mean to someone trying to understand his own situation and God's part in it.

Some five years after *Son of Man* Potter was to write *Joe's Ark*, a brave attempt to write a dry comedy about the final days of a beautiful eighteen year old Welsh girl dying of cancer. Not surprisingly the broadcast version was not a great success and the author himself came to see the difficulties involved in conveying one's own need to smash taboos even to artistic collaborators let alone audiences. Stoicism and realism in the face of tragedy can only be a matter of personal victory rather than the basis of a shared creed. That famous old royal chestnut 'Bugger Bognor' in a sense sums up the play but the humour it represents will only ever be a minority taste. Joe, the father, has great difficulty in coming to terms with his daughter's imminent death and quite understandably is irritated by the hollow clichés of his pastor, Joe Watkins, who preaches that 'all of us lack the holy imagination that could see life as the thrilling wondrous gift it really is'. The Preacher visits Joe and takes his leave by reminding him that 'Even Our Lord in his greatest agony thought that God His Father had forsaken him'. After a moment's reflection Joe shouts after the departing Preacher: 'And perhaps Our Lord was forsaken?' But matters do not rest there. Joe's position is too desperate for him to stay with that thought, he turns back to His Lord, to prayer and to the language of his faith and in Welsh he calls out for Jesus to intervene and to spare his daughter. In this interaction and in a footnote which provides an English translation of the prayer Potter explains why at this crucial moment Joe resorts to 'that strange, moaning, beleaguered tongue' rather than relying on the 'more prosaic English'. Presumably the play had been set in Wales because the playwright was all too aware of how secular a culture England had become; at least Welsh idioms still allowed for a preacher and for Biblical references to seem relevant to everyday matters (as they once had been in the Forest of Dean). This going beyond that, however, into the Welsh language itself, whilst wholly intelligible in Joe's life, also had the effect of conveying the extent to which a believer talking to his personal Saviour will have his own private language and frame of reference.

In 1976 Potter wrote *Where Adam Stood*, a play based on a small section of Edward Gosse's memoir *Father and Son*. Philip Purser has quite rightly hailed this depiction of the impact of Darwinian ideas on a Victorian scientist as 'one of the two indisputable masterpieces' written by Potter. What is pleasing about this production is that all the elements cohere. It is superbly made and the full and utterly authentic Victorian feel is guaranteed at the outset by stunning location shooting which allows us to see the sea as Victorians would have seen it and by Alan Badel's quite excellent depiction of the elder Gosse. Potter's text and Badel's Victorian air take us immediately into a world in which a living Christ and a dead mother were both very real in the lives of the Gosses, father and son. Throughout Badel ensures that we comprehend his character's combination of fundamentalist faith, intellectual authority, flippant intolerance of other people's shortcomings and growing doubts about the old shibboleths. He gives us one of the most rounded and intriguing creations in the whole of Potter's work. So satisfactory is this presentation of the Victorian Philip Gosse that it may be tempting to speculate on the degree to which Potter was benefiting from his growing skills as an adaptor for television, for in this instance he was dealing with a historical figure and with a classic Edwardian text. Of course he had been encouraged to fill out and substantiate a historical setting and intellectual context and there may have been some viewers who interpreted this as a refreshing departure from standard Potterland. This is, however, very much a Dennis Potter play and the real significance of Badel's memorable Philip Gosse is the impact he has on his young son Edmund, who during the play not only has to deal with his formidable father's varying moods, intellectual and religious dilemmas and open conviction that his son's cough could well portend an early death but also with the memory of a dead mother, an indecent assault by the local mad woman and a vision of Christ who beckons him to go who knows where. Edmund survives and he survives above all and perhaps only because he wants the model sailing ship in the shop window. Edmund has won through to a knowledge of what the survival of the fittest really means. His salvation is ensured when he calmly lies to his father with the clinching argument that 'The Good Lord says I am to have the ship'. 'Are you quite sure?', replies a father who was just prepared to put matters to the Lord on his own more usual terms. Potter was never more succinctly to convey the point that whatever the anxieties and pressures there is only one way in which they can be resolved.

In a secular era Potter continued to investigate what in his early days he had been taught was the solace of Christianity. At a time when others either ignored religion or confined it to some sort of emotional or programmed slot, he had set out to investigate what a personal faith could possibly mean in situations of stress. What remained quintessential to his treatment of Christianity was his emphasis on the paradox of belief being most needed at the very moment of weakness and despair, and so necessarily the solution and the problem become the same thing. This paradox was not unique to religion. All the while he remained aware that there were other comforts on offer, not least popular culture which for so many people had replaced organised religion. In *Where The Buffalo Roam* Potter had shown how romanticised fictions such as Western movies (increasingly fashionable for suburban intellectuals) could also become an alternative reality for those denied emotional support and maturity at home and in school. We had been left in no doubt as to the immediate attractions of a world in which one expected to be called 'Shane' but the trouble was that within that world solutions had seemed too readily at hand. A bid for freedom had come to a violent end. This was always the danger for someone not able to comprehend the degree to which they had been seduced by an unreal substitute. Potter's fullest examination of this syndrome came in his 1969 play *Moonlight on The Highway* in which a fairly straightforward story line is encumbered with an enormous load of complex psychological assumptions and is only meaningfully sustained by the intensity of Ian Holm's acting. Written at the close of rock music's great decade, the play concerns a young man who edits a roneo'd newsletter devoted to the career of the artist he regards as 'the greatest singer ever'. The singer is now dead and so the young man's flat becomes a shrine to his memory, dominated by a poster and the sounds of his records. A television programme is to be made about the great singer and our young man is to be interviewed; there is a rally to commemorate the singer, a film to be shown and our young man is to be a keynote speaker. Quite simply Potter has faithfully recreated the kind of world inhabited by millions of young fans of contemporary music in the 1960s, but of course he had chosen a dead artist in part to make more obvious the many connections between popular music and Christianity. The young man, Peters, played by Ian Holm, could just as easily have belonged to an evangelical sect as to his appreciation society. As it happens (and in a moment we will see why) Potter had chosen Al Bowlly, the crooner killed in 1941, to be the musician at the centre of his play without fully realising the extent to which the new phenomenon of prematurely dead rock idols was to be a feature of the decades ahead. Astonishingly, Potter had anticipated the dead Elvis phenomenon and he had done this because he was less interested in what appeared to be the fashions of the 1960s than he was in the question of what those who were psychologically crippled wanted from their chosen cults.

Peters is certainly crippled. His father was killed by a V2 in 1945; his mother survived but with only one foot and with a domineering nature. Now she is recently dead and the son confesses that he 'didn't love her — she kept me on a piece of string'. Perhaps her death has precipitated a real crisis for Peters and we become the witnesses of that. Increasingly he is troubled by the memory of being sexually assaulted at the age of ten by a man with spikey hair, possibly a tramp: he relives the horror of how the walls of a chocolate factory nullified his cries of 'Mummie, Mummie!'. We see him curse his landlord, who is another real cripple, we see him attempt to assault the attractive television reporter who comes to interview him and then confess to an uncomprehending psychiatrist that he knows that he is 'wicked'. By instalments we gather that Peters' problem is sexual, that somehow as his name might suggest he is incapable of a mature relationship. Finally at the rally he reveals that he has slept with 136 tarts. All the while of course, we have been listening to the sweet tones of Al Bowlly and learning too of the immense responsibility of his musical legacy as far as Peters is concerned. In part Bowlly's songs just represent childhood innocence and happiness. As it happens Bowlly too was killed in the Blitz 'by the bloody Krauts' and that just emphasises how much he is associated with a time before things went wrong. But over and above that Peters is not capable of mature love and loving sex and so Bowlly's sentiments in those respects become the ideal and the only context in which those things can be meaningfully comprehended and accepted. At one level Peters is just nostalgic but his complaint that the present age was one of 'vulgarity' is far more than a matter of taste, for every aspect of the post-Bowlly, post-family-happiness days is vulgar, not least its sexuality. For Peters, Bowlly makes sex sound lovely, in fact 'not like sex at all', and his lyrics are not just conceits but, far more, heartfelt truths. "Lover Where Can You Be?" is what Peters asks in the loneliness of his apartment and "You Can't Buy Love" is the lesson that he has bitterly learnt.

We are looking at plays in which Dennis Potter was deliberately writing against the expectations of his generation and certainly of the set of which he had seemed very much a part until his enforced return to the West. At the time, though, it was doubtful that the measure of his rejection and rebellion was fully appreciated. In general he was thought of as being rather naughty in the ways of the late 1950s and 1960s, an angry young man who was still going on about the same old preoccupations that had inspired that initial rebellion. It was quite rare for critics or viewers to fully contemplate the implications of Potterland; rather he was just thought of as someone taking advantage of the new liberalism and permissiveness. At that stage comparatively little was known of Potter and certainly there was no obvious prompting for his plays to be considered on his terms. Writers had now been given a certain license and so shocks were all part of the new diet offered to what was now regarded as a more mature television audience. Above all sexual explicitness was now almost *de rigueur* for serious and, what was really the same thing, naturalistic drama. Perhaps it was even the hallmark of good drama. Potter was increasingly thought of as giving good value as a television dramatist because he guarateed hot scenes. His six-part *Casanova*, which is remembered in one history of television as having offered 'a succession of actresses in varying degrees of undress', was very largely responsible for that reputation.

In the heady days of sixties and seventies television a sex scene was evidence enough for most intellectuals that a play was breaking down the mediocrity and oppression of convention and was in general a liberating force. Only gradually did the realisation come that Dennis Potter had been registering a protest against the era's all too easy sexuality. This had been particularly the case with

Casanova. These were times that did not want to know about the other side of sex and one well recalls the disorientation caused by the movie *Alfie* in which those who wanted to treasure the charm of Michael Caine fought hard to suppress the memory of Vivien Merchant's abortion. It took quite a while before what Potter was saying about sex was put in any context.

Even Philip Purser, Potter's earliest champion, clearly had difficulty with the majority of the author's plays written in this period. Purser identified a group of plays and a novel which dealt primarily with the interplay between a writer and his characters and a further group that dealt with particular families having to come to terms with the specific identity of a visiting stranger. In his essay Purser talked of these works as belonging to distinct groups not least because of cross-references, repetitions and a preoccupation with the same ideas, jokes and relationships, rather than with newly minted characters or situations. There is no masterpiece here, no one play which is totally satisfactory, and Purser is right to imply that they all have the feel of being interim episodes of a larger work in progress. He talks of a playwright as 'settling a few old scores' as he deals with contemporary television and of the whole question of the relationship between an author and his work as being 'too private a metaphysical concern'. Although Purser discusses the sexual content of specific plays what he did not do in his groundbreaking essay was to indicate the extent to which sexual tension and anxieties formed by far the most obvious theme and that generally those anxieties are attributed to characters who were contemporary middle-class intellectuals. *Angels Are So Few* was the most controversial television play of 1970 and in it we see an unhappy married couple watching a television programme about the making of a blue movie. Three years later came *Only Make Believe* in which the action concerns the degree to which the author of a television play, which happens to be *Angels Are So Few*, draws on his own experiences. Meanwhile in *Follow The Yellow Brick Road* (1972) the central character Jack Black is an actor who is having a nervous breakdown and who thinks that his visit to a psychiatrist is his latest acting job. We are shown some pretty dreadful commercials but still Jack prefers them to the general run of television plays which he denounces furiously for they 'turn love into sticky slime' and are written by

'Trotskyites who go to parties and pass the clap on to each other like a baton'. Certainly *Yellow Brick Road* was meant to invite a contemplation of the relationship between commercials and televised drama and of what both were doing to contemporary lifestyles but Jack Black was no mere television critic. The key to his breakdown is that he has seen his wife in bed with another man and soon he learns that she has also committed adultery with his agent. He denounces his wife as 'a bitch on heat' and turns away from her 'stench'; later he hits and kicks her. He visits the agent's wife and tells her how he has always admired her purity and innocence. But for all her Snow White schoolgirl qualities she too turns out to be a vamp. Sitting in bed in a white nightie eating biscuits, her response to his hopeless idealism is to say 'I always knew you fancied me'; meanwhile her newly acquired poodle pees on the whiter than white carpet. In *Schmoedipus* (1974) a young man introduces himself to a housewife as her long-lost son but it transpires that he is far more a product of her desire and of her guilt than of her womb, whilst in *Double Dare* (1976) an actress to whom a troubled writer is attracted not only makes suggestive adverts but is indistinguishable from a prostitute whom we see at her trade.

In these years, then, Potter was working away at several basic notions about sex, aiming for more honesty and complexity than that found in the general fictions of the period. For his settings he relied on his own circumstances as a writer and on the world of television in which he had once worked and which remained the basis of his professional being. Even as he makes his protest and earns his living he is broadening out and deepening themes that were basic to his identity as a writer. There were some terrific moments in these plays and all the time the author could rely on highly charged and intelligent acting but within the single play format there was always the feeling that we do not know enough about the central characters to fully absorb all the psychological information and references with which we are bombarded. Perhaps Potter was aware of constraints because out of this work there appeared his first novel and Purser was spot on in placing *Hide and Seek* in this context. Here both Potter and his readers have the luxury of time and space. In addition the writer could be more explicit even as he developed more subtle distancing techniques.

As indicated earlier *Hide and Seek* is the crucial guide-book to Potterland. The game that Potter the novelist plays, first with his character Daniel Miller who thinks that he might be a character in somebody else's story and then with an author who is trying to decide what to make of Daniel, is always intriguing and amusing but it is the sexual dimension that binds the whole book together. Like so many Potter works of this period the story starts with a patient confronting uncomprehending doctors; as usual these men in white coats are denied sophistication and insight. What Daniel Miller has to try to convey to the doctors is that not only is he to be a character in a book but it's 'a dirty book', one 'peopled with foul creatures, stained flesh, dirty pictures, faithless women with rotting cunts, sucking mouths'. Into his mind comes memories of frequent sex with prostitutes and of hitting his wife, but above all there are earlier memories of something having happened in the woods of his childhood, and of his parents having sex and leaving tell-tale love bites on his mother's neck. Most confusing was his difficulty in identifying the women in his life: 'How many times had he woken with the wrong name in his mouth?'. Whom was he addressing as he seeks reassurance, 'dead mother or separated wife?'.

We come to understand more when we meet the author who has created Daniel Miller and who gave him his illness. The Author had chosen psoriatic arthropathy because it was a 'nasty ailment' that conveniently showed 'how the guilt or evil in his mind finds physical expression in and on his body'. It was a 'pestilence' proving that 'he who touches pitch shall be indelibly stained with pitch'. Daniel may deny such abominations 'as hitting his wife or putting his penis in a prostitute's dribbling mouth' but 'what the flapping tongue denies the pain-scorched limbs confirm'. Later it is the Author himself who recalls particular prostitutes: there was the beautiful Sandra from the Forest of Dean whose first commercial transaction had been with her step-father and whose mother's advice had been 'Doesn't thou ever give it away for nothing o' butty'. There had been the girl from Guyana with whom he had sex whilst her young son slept a few feet away. There was also the childhood memory of the Italian man who had robbed him of his sexual innocence in the Forest of Dean. In spite of these memories the Author has preserved warm and tender feelings for women;

he can see the Angel and the Snow White in them, but it is the thought of the sexual act that disgusts him and which inspires a tirade against 'spoiled human flesh':

> 'Mouth upon mouth, tongue against tongue, limb upon limb, skin rubbing at skin. Faces contort and organs spout out a smelly stain, a sticky betrayal. The crudest joke against the human race lies in that sweaty farce by which we are first formed and given life.... We are spat out of fevered loins, or punctured rubber, or drunken grapplings in creaking beds.'

A new generation had been taught that sexual pleasure was not only a fundamental human right to be claimed as early and as often as possible, but also that it was essentially a form of truth. Sexual prohibition was the worst kind of authoritarian suppression and sexual inhibitions the cowardice of the mediocre and irrelevant. For reactionaries and fuddy-duddies, all of those who advocated or depicted sex were revolutionaries of a new order and Potter was long thought of as belonging to that *avant-garde*. The objections to him were against his explicitness rather than the blackness of his preoccupations. The great divide of the era was between those who would celebrate and expose the body beautiful and those who would conceal it. What Potter had been investigating was how the body and mind could be crippled by sexual guilt, and the question he was now always probing was where relief was to be found for that man who could hardly stand the thought that all women (however we choose to see them) have sexual appetites, and for whom childhood memories have prescribed that the sexual act, however necessary, can only be experienced with a sense of disgust. At this stage nobody was yet asking many questions about Potter as an autobiographical writer, but already it was evident that he was fascinated by and experimenting with the problem of how this sexual syndrome could be dramatized or fictionalized and that he was undoubtedly involved in a process of trial and error in which he was aiming for the correct balance between immediate and recollected action, even as he took greater risks in what he could reveal and get away with.

In so many ways he was pushing his luck and things in the shape of the establishment caught up with him as he presented the BBC with his 1976 play *Brimstone and Treacle*. The play which had cost £70,000 to make was banned by Alasdair Milne, Director of Programmes, because he found it 'nauseating' and he was sure audiences would find revolting the scenes in which a girl who had been reduced by a car accident to the state of a vegetable is raped by a visitor whom we are led to believe may be the devil. The play was not shown for eleven years, but meanwhile the text was there to be read, the tape was viewed by various select audiences, there was a stage production and in 1983 a film version. As the play was analysed and debated so there was considerable speculation as to the identity of the visitor, and as to why it was precisely that his violation of the girl seemingly brings her back to her senses. This paradox is really the blackest of black jokes and as the devil strikes we can but compare his method to the hours of devoted and yet futile nursing that the parents had provided over the years since the accident. The whole play is really a comedy about the suburban hopelessness of the parents: they are so dull, so caught up in clichés, so rooted to the television, and all the while they intensify their political illiberalism, a tendency which the visitor will eagerly encourage. In his text Potter emphasises their pathetic social pretension; they make real coffee and like *boeuf bourguignon* 'properly made of course'. We gather that the mother, Mrs Bates, is religious and in the film version Potter develops this theme by making Mr Bates a religous publisher and writer of commemorative verses; even his religion has been reduced to clichés. What we have, then, is a very ordinary suburban family whose whole existence is now dominated by a central tragedy, which is largely beyond their comprehensions, especially as doctors suggest that the daughter's condition is one of trauma rather than of purely physical damage. But Potter has not just written a black comedy of the inadequate in the face of the desperate, for it transpires that the daughter had been knocked down by a car as she fled from a glimpse of her father having sex with one of her friends. The car was in effect irrelevant; it was the father who had plunged his daughter into shock. In one of the most extreme forms imaginable Mr Bates has been punished for his infidelity and betrayal and, as for his wife, whose only possible shortcoming could have been a lack of warmth for her husband, she has been made to pay an even greater price as the real job of nursing falls on her. Whoever the stranger may be his message is one of love: this is the only thing that can save young Pattie and by implication, of course, her parents too. 'We live in the shadows — and we can see no light' is how Mr Bates sums up their miserable existence, and it is precisely the light of love that the stranger preaches. But then he rapes the girl. The point here, of course, is not the viciousness or intensity of his sexual urge but rather that it is only by forcing Pattie and Mr Bates through that memory of a particular copulation that barriers can be brought down. In the film version the daughter's first words as her consciousness returns are addressed to her father: 'How could you and with that woman?'. What the devil's visit has done is to facilitate the making of the accusation. The whole family, but the father in particular, have openly to confront the actual nature of the betrayal, the lie, the sin that had become the cornerstone of their miserable existence.

The Bates family had to be made to pass through the actual moment that had precipitated the tragedy, and this passage of theirs towards the moment of truth can be taken as the major theme of Dennis Potter's work in this decade. The great irony, of course, was that the playwright whose name had become synonymous with sexual explicitness had seemingly been driven to write by the notion that sex could be sinful and that the subsequent guilt could lead to both mental and physical illness in which the possibilities of normal mature sex and love were impaired, and which could well lead to violence. He had been all the while writing against the grain of his times and juxtaposing the naive belief that opportunity could only lead to fulfilment with the more pessimistic view that availing oneself could be one's very undoing. Free love had been the credo of a generation and there were some who saw Potter, and particularly his Casanova (as played by Frank Finlay), as a highpriest of that cause whereas all the while, even (he felt) with *Casanova*, he had been examining those circumstances and actions that could undermine and destroy the purity of sex and its need to be unambiguously associated with love. His voice had been a jarring one but almost incredibly that point had not been fully taken up within the culture because superficially his preoccupations seemed to be so contemporary. To write about sex was to be contemporary but what made him seem even more so was that his plays dealt with television, with advertising and with conspicuous consumption amongst the new artistic élite. Throughout the decade his preoccupation with the evils of mass manipulation and affluence had always been emphasised more than his puritan's notion of sin. His socialist critique of the suburbs and the studios had allowed people to ignore his old-fashioned preacher's voice. The text of *Brimstone and Treacle*, which was published in 1978, carried on its cover a quotation from *The Guardian* telling audiences that they will see 'the guilty faith of the instinctive rationalist' and 'the born socialist's comprehension of the rancorous sourness of the middle-class'. Here as always the social critique is played up and little is made of the fact that the play is plunging us back into the moral world of the Old Testament.

The effect of the 1960s had been to release waves of fashion, to create patterns of creative and consumer expectation and Potter, whatever his own immediate preoccupation, had been swept along on that tide. His own early career had been at the very centre of the new in-scene and he had chosen to work in the medium of television, by now very much the arbiter of middle-class taste. Now a work of his was banned from the screen because it might offend viewers. There were few, it was assumed, who could take the actual depiction of a comatose girl being raped. But how many were there prepared to discuss the reality of sin, especially in the context of sex, let alone the need for atonement? In the privacy of the author's study the rape of Pattie had seemed the absolutely right development in what had been a long preoccupation, but the resulting ban fully indicated the huge gap there was between his private thought process and the concept of what constituted entertainment. Perhaps with Mr Bates and his daughter Potter had gone as far as he could with agony in the suburbs of the television age. He had created a brilliant *coup de télévision* to convey the way in which sin could be expiated but it had not been acceptable let alone discussed for what it really meant. Perhaps the time had come to change his ground somewhat, to place the problem in a slightly different context. The four-square quality of *A Beast With Two Backs* and the perfection of *Where Adam Stood* had shown how Potter's Biblical sense of transgression and affliction could work in a historical context and, of course, his very successful career as an adaptor of Thomas Hardy was winning him over to the concept of the mini-series which he had already explored with *Casanova* (in 1971) and *Late Call* (in 1975). And so it was that *Pennies From Heaven* was conceived. The theology and psychology were the same and as always Potter was to offend the same old campaigners against permissivness and explicitness but now there was a sureness of touch, a pleasingness, a warmth and a sheer sense of entertainment which convinced producers, critics and a mass audience that here was a master of the craft of television drama. From the fringe the author now moved to the centre of what was very much a national television culture.

Pennies From Heaven was undoubtedly the great turning-point in Potter's career. It gave him a mass following, made his name a bankable commodity and finally convinced critics that he was a classic source of genuinely imaginative and creative television. When the mini-series was repeated on American television in 1989 the *New York Times* critic John J. O'Connor reminded his readers that Potter and his production team were offering 'a world as enchanting and terrifying and magical as that of any fairy tale' and providing 'an outstanding example of how television itself can be a distinctive art form whose true potential is still being realised only sporadically'. From the very beginning both audiences and critics alike had been aware that they were being exposed to a new kind of television experience, and what caught their attention most and made the programmes a great conversation piece was the author's technique of having the characters step out of the naturalistic story to "lip-sync" popular songs of the period before returning to the scene where they had left it. What made this device seem so appropriate was the fact that the story concerned the fate of Arthur, a cockney sheet-music salesman who ventures out from London in the grim days of the 1930s to sell his songs to provincial store-keepers. The music itself was delightful: Potter used some sixty original recordings from the 1930s, many of them by the crooner Al Bowlly. The success of the series was in very great part due to the music and, as Philip Purser pointed out, the proof of that came in the great revival of Dance Band music with the records of the *Pennies From Heaven* soundtrack prominent in the new sales pitch. Potter had undoubtedly alighted on an immensely pleasing formula which had allowed what had been a somewhat concealed nostalgia for the 1930s to come out into the open. This raises the question, though, of whether audiences were reacting to the music in the way the author had intended, whether they had fully appreciated why this particular device had been chosen. Perhaps it may even be argued that this possible misunderstanding over the tunes was part of a wider misunderstanding of the whole story. Potter had succeeded as a television playwright as never before, but perhaps the new acclaim had accrued in spite of, rather than because of, his message.

The whole action of the story is dominated by the character of Arthur as created by Bob Hoskins. This was a very brilliant performance by an actor for whom this part was the stepping-stone to both national and international fame. Hoskins was absolutely right for Arthur and perhaps the series would have made far less impact without him so wholeheartedly to sustain the momentum and tension of the story. Above all it is Hoskins who legitimises the music, for here is a little man, an ordinary man, and yet somebody whose energy, idealism and essential optimism entitle him to aspire to better and different things. He has already made it to the affluent suburbs but surely now his belief in his own powers and his product will see him through to even better things in spite of the obstacles in his way — his wife's generally negative approach to life (including sex), the caution of shopkeepers and the difficulty of the times. It is Hoskins' Cockney cheerfulness and positive determination to win through that attracts us fully to his side and we in turn love the music and appreciate it afresh because it so neatly captures his energies. When he sets off along the A40 to Gloucestershire to the tune of "Prairie Moon" we want him to succeed with the formidable task of selling happy upbeat music in that provincial 'desert'. We know exactly how he feels when "Zing Went The Strings Of My Heart" breaks out as he meets an attractive girl in a pub; and why shouldn't he have sex with his wife (to the tune of "We'll Make Hay While The Sun Shines") on the counter of his new record shop which he hopes will be 'a little gold mine'? But there is a real sadness in Hoskins' performance too and its most stunning aspect is the way in which for all his energy and optimism he always seems to be on the verge of shedding tears of disappointment. The sex his wife offers is grudging and frigid and so we appreciate the irony and plaintiveness of "Someday If Luck Is Kind", "Somewhere The Sun Is Shining" and "Down Sunny Side Lane", and above all we understand the very moving pathos of the great speech in Episode Two as Arthur fully realises the comforting role of the songs he sells. They really are *Pennies From Heaven*, but now in addition the songs are coming true; Eileen, the girl he has just met in a pub, has seen to that.

Much of the series worked on this level; we associate with the Cockney salesman determined to fulfil himself in the 1930s. Much of this seemed absolutely right and rang so true. We are offered a revisionist view of the thirties because in the popular mind the decade was one of privation rather than improvement, but Potter has achieved absolute historical authenticity. This was a boom time for London and this particular story is at the outset firmly rooted in the new affluent suburbs, and both the animated title sequence and the set establish the splendour of Arthur's detached home with its stained glass, electric lights, lace curtains and radio. Arthur's wife belongs entirely to the world of coffee-mornings, teashops and door-to-door salesmen. This was a new consumer age and the self-made self-improving Arthur with his Cockney roots and his Tin-Pan Alley songs is a perfectly selected representative of all the positive aspirations and energies that were taking Britain out of the Depression. We can award full marks then for historical verisimilitude and in this respect we can disregard Philip Purser's objection that the series smacked too much of the mythical 1930s as represented in Great Western Railway posters. There is undoubtedly a strip-cartoon aproach to the period throughout the series, but that helps to give the narrative pace and in any case the authenticity of the acting and the wit of the dialogue always prevent the danger of caricature and stereotype. The story of Arthur and his mistress Eileen as created by Bob Hoskins and Cheryl Campbell is a real and convincing treatment of the themes of improvement and aspiration in that period before the Second World War. But however much that helps explain our enjoyment and acceptance of what is on offer that is not Dennis Potter's point, for he wants to punish Arthur and Eileen for their striving and furthermore he insists that the music which seems so appropriate to their yearnings was very significantly to blame for their weaknesses and eventual ruination.

DENNIS POTTER

The playwright had set out to write a tragedy, albeit one punctured by considerable wit and humour. In the end he probably thought that he had done his job too well for Arthur is allowed to come back from the dead to join his grieving lover. He becomes then the final "penny from heaven" and the message is that "The Song Has Ended But The Melody Lingers On". This final anti-naturalistic twist is unnecessary and unconvincing for Hoskins' acting and the music itself would have assured on their own that the "death where is thy sting" dimension was understood. Potter should have recalled all those Hollywood movies when audiences were less interested in the conventional studio-imposed endings, than in the charismatic acting of the stars. Whatever the trite ending the fact remains that Arthur has been executed for a murder he did not commit and his mistress is essentially bereft. Why have they been punished? Why does their world fall apart? The answers to those questions are not straighforward. Arthur, of course, is a victim and overall we are left in no doubt that we should have sympathy for him. His wife is middle-class, the daughter of a wealthy father and she has obviously sold out entirely to the consumerism of the suburbs. She is superficial, attracted by surfaces, images, symbols, and incapable of sharing her husband's enthusiasm or of responding to his need for passionate sex. She is essentially a child, happy with the toys her wealth allows her to acquire but incapable of understanding the great forces at work in the world outside her kitchen. Arthur is a victim too of society; shopkeepers and customers alike are unable to share his enthusiasm for the new music and for gramophone records. He loves his field of work but it is one in which there are 'too many middlemen'. At the end he is the victim of an establishment court, a chamber riddled with middle-class hypocrites all too prepared to assume him guilty because of his lack of pedigree. These external forces are stacked against Arthur but even more he is a victim of his own weaknesses. Surely his sexual appetite is too great — and perhaps abnormal? He not only "wants it regular" from his wife, he also wants her to put lipstick on her nipples and to go around without knickers. 'On a dark night', says Arthur, 'I sometimes think I'd fuck my own grandmother'. And so he begins the affair that comes to dominate his life and begins it very appropriately by lying about his job and his marital status.

He now finds real passion, and indeed love, but all this happiness is illicit and by implication too much of an indulgence; there will be a price to pay. The author's charges against Arthur are mounting but still the indictment is not complete. Eventually Arthur is to be executed for a crime he did not commit but nonetheless there is a scene in which he does confront the beautiful blind girl, who is soon to be found dead. In an amazing scene Bob Hoskins as Arthur looks at the girl and an appreciation of her beauty, then pity, then lust, all flash through his mind and across his face. For a moment he wants to take her knickers off and indeed for a moment we wonder whether he actually does this before killing her. In other words the playwright makes Arthur guilty of the thought. Perhaps he is an animal, 'a filthy beast' in his wife's words. Perhaps he deserves to go to the gallows. He obviously has very little self-restraint and perhaps that is why the songs are so important in shaping his life. "Roll Me Over In The Clover", sings a man in a pub and, reflects Arthur, 'That's what all the songs are about'. He confesses later that for him sex 'is the main thing, isn't it?' and Eileen tells him that inevitably there was an element of fantasy in their affair for 'you acted as if the songs were real, as though you'd written them yourself'.

To a considerable extent Arthur is a victim of his circumstances and of his own nature and the same is true of his partner in the adventure, Eileen. When we meet her she is obviously a very sympathetic and successful schoolteacher who tells charming fairy tales to her Forest of Dean classes and teaches them that all things are 'bright and beautiful', though she lives in a fairly brutal world where she is entirely taken for granted by her coalmining father and brother who are dependent on her to run their home now the mother is dead. They are quite capable of humiliating her in front of her children, of making her the victim of cruel practical jokes and of demeaning her profession: 'call that a job?', they jibe. She is ready to be rescued and so falls for the charming Londoner who first lies to her and then ravishes her on her own kitchen floor. She drifts to London in search of the Arthur who has abandoned her and is soon made aware that sex is largely a commercial commodity on the streets of the capital. She is driven to prostitution so as to survive and be able to pay for an abortion. She meets Arthur again and their passion is rekindled. He is now prepared to leave his wife for her but in so doing he becomes dependent on her immoral earnings. They are totally caught up in adventure now and she seems prepared to accept their fate. They learn that he is wanted for murder and go into hiding, and when an eccentric farmer forces them to make love in front of him she shoots the farmer because she 'felt like it' and realises now that they might as well be hanged together. Eileen's story is an amazing one and one almost wishes that it could be told separately with her as the lead subject. But inevitably in this telling of the tale she is here as an adjunct to Arthur and all too often she is made to do things and say things for the sake of the plot rather than the logic of her own character. Cheryl Campbell is perky enough in the part but never quite knows how naive or all-knowing her character should be. Even her Dean accent comes and goes. Above all, of course, she contributes to the notion that this pair have to be punished. She has had sex with a stranger, she has abandoned her home, she quite obviously enjoys sex even when she is doing it for money, and in the end it is she who willingly commits murder as she begins to comprehend the degree of male hypocrisy and perversity.

Over six episodes we are made fully aware of the many forces that interact to destroy Arthur and Eileen and in a sense the whole logic of the piece is that they are inevitably doomed. The process is inexorable and at every stage they are trapped by new circumstances either of their own or of a hostile society's making. The drama of growing inevitability can be quite fascinating and rewarding, especially here where the external forces are made to interact so neatly with the personality weaknesses of the central characters. We know they are doomed and we accept each snare and trap that cuts off any hope of their success and salvation. But isn't there occasionally a small voice within us that asks why this is happening? They are in so many ways an attractive and sympathetic couple. There is something immensely appealing about Arthur, the man who longs to be able to play a musical instrument ('even the mouth organ'), who in his fantasies wears a tuxedo and conducts his own band as they play "You And The Night And The Music". Even as things are he is enormously proud of his taste and professional expertise as a musical salesman; he is someone who 'can tell a dog when he hears one'.

1. The Pupil and the Teacher. Keith Barron and Janet Henfrey in *Stand Up, Nigel Barton* (1965)

2. The 'V' Sign. Keith Barron as Nigel Barton in *Vote, Vote, Vote for Nigel Barton* (1965)

3. The National Serviceman. Nikolas Simmonds at the opening of
Lay Down Your Arms (1970)

4. Mother and Son. Hywel Bennet and Megs Jenkins in
Where The Buffalo Roam (1966)

6. A Son Forsaken. Colin Blakely as Christ in *Son of Man* (1969)

5. Father and Son. Denis Carey and Christian Rodska in *The Beast With Two Backs* (1968).

7. A Father to be Challenged, Alan Badel as Philip Gosse in *Where Adam Stood* (1976) and 8. The Erring Father, Denholm Elliott introduces Sting as Martin to the other members of the Bates family, Joan Plowright is the mother and Suzanne Hamilton the daughter in the movie version of *Brimstone and Treacle* (1982)

9. The Salesman *par excellence*. Bob Hoskins as Arthur Parker in *Pennies From Heaven* (1978), and 10. The *Alter Ego*, Kenneth Colley as the Accordian Man in the same play.

11. The Children of *Blue Remembered Hills* (1979). The cast was Colin Jeavens (Donald Duck), Michael Elphick (Peter), Janine Duvitski (Audrey), Colin Welland (Willie), Robin Ellis (John), John Bird (Raymond) and Helen Mirren (Angela).

12. The Parents. Jim Carter and Alison Steadman as Mr & Mrs Marlow, and Patrick Malahide (left) as Binney, revealed as the lover at the moment of truth in *The Singing Detective* (1986).

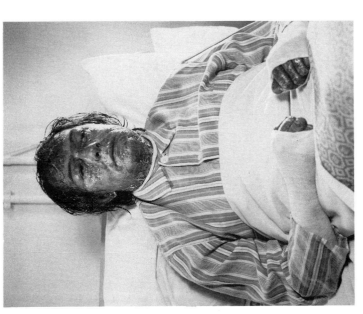

13. The Patient and 14. The Detective. Michael Gambon as Marlow in *The Singing Detective* (1986).

16. 'You gotta live, haven't yuh!': The Survivor. Louise Germaine as Sylvia with Douglas Henshall as Peter in *Lipstick On Your Collar* (1993).

15. The Model and The Author. Gina Bellman as Blackeyes and Michael Gough as Kingsley (1989).

Eileen too is obviously first-class at her job and she has lots of bounce and wit that should have guaranteed her success in any career. As a couple they have much to offer and have exactly the kind of personalities and ambitions that should have brought success in the Britain of the 1930s. Why then are they doomed? There was nothing wrong with their aspirations. The implication is that they were too ambitious, that they seemed to think that success and happiness were theirs by right. But surely those things in themselves would not seem to warrant extreme punishment and Potter obviously knows that, which is why he comes to rely on so many separate forces of destruction. Dramatically he needs his inexorable process but there is often the sense that no single indictment has really been enough to clinch their demise. In interviews Potter was to make much of the music and the way in which it showed how people could 'get into a mess' because of the tension between their yearning for wholeness and the actual circumstances of their lives. Years later he was to tell Patrick Wright that the songs in *Pennies From Heaven* were there as 'a cheap lie': Arthur 'believes the world can be other than it is, but this is a sort of fake transcendence, a kind of tawdriness'. The intention was clearly to suggest that the love of popular music shared by Arthur and Eileen fuelled their sense of frustration having promised them that happiness was an easily obtainable right. But is that really how we see it? Has the author rather misunderstood and underestimated his own characters? Just as evident is the fact that the music acts as solace for the two lovers and also helps to give them a sense of style, personal dignity and purpose. It confirms their sense of being special and gives them additional energy. The music is fabulous and perhaps they were enjoying it in precisely the same ways as the viewer. One might resent the suggestion that they are in a mess because of the music, and quite clearly the author does not want to make too much of that because the indictment against them is built up on many other fronts as well. In each instance, however, one wonders whether it is enough.

On the face of it no man deserves to go to the gallows because he asks his wife to paint her nipples and to go without her knickers. Neither would there seem to be a moral case for capital punishment for a man who has an affair even if he does subsequently abandon the girl. Potter knows this but he is constructing stepping stones on the way to greater iniquity. Ultimately Arthur is guilty of having evil thoughts about a young blind girl and then of deserting his wife, but neither are these capital offences. He has been foolish and has lived dangerously but perhaps he deserved to get away with it, especially as he has ended up with a girl to whom he is so well suited. Why couldn't Arthur and Eileen win through to domestic bliss with, say, a successful business in Gloucester and a charming house in the Cotswolds? Many people will have got away with more. But there is to be no escape and so eventually, and not entirely satisfactorily, Potter resorts to class. Ultimately Arthur and Eileen are victims of a privileged system. Eileen does, in fact, become a murderess and we are asked to accept this somewhat unnecessary and gratuitous crime which is perhaps very much out of character as an understandable response to male hypocrisy and sexuality, for having been the favourite prostitute of an establishment MP she is now made to make love publicly for a farmer who assumes that she and Arthur must be Gypsies or Jews. There are heavy class overtones at the end as the Court just assumes that Arthur, the little man, is guilty. Yet why is he hanged? For everything or for just one thing?

Potter wants it all ways — perhaps too many ways. The inevitability and the interrelatedness of the plot intrigue and fascinate but in part one resents the stigma that is attached to aspiration and to romantic music as well as the implication that sexual appetite, infidelity and lascivious thoughts demand punishment. The author stacks the odds and does so in ways that suggest that he personally resents the very energies and freedom that he has given his characters. The tension in this play grows out of our realisation that the author has doomed the lovers whereas we not only want them to succeed but also suspect that they really had the resources to have won through. Frequently in interviews Potter was to do Arthur down by talking of his tawdry dreams and of his uneducated, naive and stupid belief that the songs could in any way be real. One really begins to wonder if the author is being fair to or really understands his own creation. But ultimately the issue of Arthur's resources is irrelevant.

Our hopes and wishes are to be of no avail, for the God-like author sticks to his predestined plan. This is ultimately as Calvinist a tale as one is ever likely to encounter and Potter could not resist the temptation to add his own personal theological dimension. Arthur and Eileen never had a chance, as there were forces at work that were far more powerful than bourgeois MPs, policemen and judges, forces that they would never recognise and comprehend. The blind girl was actually murdered by an accordion-playing itinerant tramp. As acted by Kenneth Colley the tramp is given an astonishingly ascetic, not to say Christ-like, air and his stock-in-trade are dirge-like renditions of "The Old Rugged Cross" and "Rock Of Ages". Who is he and what does he represent? He plays an alternative popular music and clearly the suggestion is that the paradise he peddles is as misleading, unrealistic and dangerous as that offered by Arthur. In later years Potter was to write of his hatred of the false promises made in the hymns of Ira Sankey, hymns that he had sung on every Sunday of his childhood. At first Arthur dimisses the accordion man as a 'half-wit' but then he embraces him as a fellow labourer in the field. They are both purveyors of cheap and easy dreams as lies. But that is by no means all, for in embracing this holy fool Arthur is embracing his fate. This is the man who will send him to the gallows and his tragic significance is indicated by his presence at that moment when Arthur meets Eileen. She is first seen in the ritzy music shop where Arthur is trying to sell his songs but then she leaves and Arthur, hearing a rendition of "There Is A Green Hill Far Away", looks out and sees her standing and listening to the accordion man right under the massive presence of Gloucester Cathedral. The accordion man finishes his tune and then switches to "Rock Of Ages, Cleft For Me", a hymn whose words call upon Christ to let the water and the blood which flowed from His side 'be of sin the double cure' so that any appellant can be saved from 'its guilt and power'. 'Foul I to the fountain fly', the cry continues, 'Wash me Saviour or I die'. The accordion man/tramp is later to flit in and out of the story; we see him having a frightening fit, then having a nightmare as he realizes he has killed the girl. Eventually he drowns himself in the Thames. He becomes the thinnest and merest of sub-plots, the virtual stranger who, as luck would have it, occasions Arthur's demise. But at that initial moment in Gloucester he was something more than that: an idiot perhaps, Fate certainly, but someone whose message should not have been so lightly dismissed. Arthur and Eileen are about to sin, they are foul.

DENNIS POTTER

For all their charm, energy and wit they have no hope. They will
not be washed; they will die.

Pennies From Heaven is a powerful story; the author had been well
served by the director Piers Haggard and the production team.
Hoskins had turned in a great performance and the music had
done its work and in so doing taken on a new lease of life. It was
not surprising that Hollywood should sit up and take notice and
within three years there was a movie version of the story which,
according to the credits, was written for the screen and based on
original material by Dennis Potter. The story is now transferred to
the America of the 1930s. The Hollywood effort is very worthwhile
and obviously quite fascinating for viewers familiar with the
original. John J. O'Connor was to dismiss it as a mediocre film but
many critics on both sides of the Atlantic welcomed it as a
refreshing, intelligent American story. Unfortunately it did badly
at the box-office, partly because MGM were never quite sure how
to market it but mainly because the mass American audience
prefers films that respect the strict conventions of genre and
dislikes being reminded of some of the grubbier facts of life. Here
again Arthur bounces back from the dead to reassure Eileen and
us that 'we could not go through all that and not have a happy
ending'. This is even weaker than the ending in the original and
in any case did nothing to erase the unpleasant experience audiences had been given of illicit sex, abortion, prostitution, murder
and broken dreams. The great irony, of course, was that Potter's
story was authentically American and in the movie version he was
using the music far more legitimately in the social and cultural
context that had first inspired it. In fact to see the movie is to realise
the extent to which Potter had been influenced by American
popular culture and had conceived his original English story in
the American idiom. The transfer, then, is utterly natural and we
can see the film as a mix of the 1930s social problem film (the Paul
Muni of *I Am a Fugitive From a Chain Gang* would have been perfect
as Arthur) and the classic Depression musical in which the young
girl from the boondocks is about to break into a Broadway show
(the Eileen of the film, Bernadette Peters, is a Ruby Keeler lookalike
and there are strong echoes of *42nd Street*). The period atmosphere
is clinched by the way in which sets, locations and costumes were
based on those classic images of Thirties America that had been

100

created by the painter Edward Hopper and the photographer Walker Evans. The trouble is, of course, that all this authenticity and legitimacy somewhat weaken the impact of the story. The original English story had been historically authentic but nevertheless it had contributed a revisionist or certainly a somewhat neglected perspective on a chapter of social history. Now, with his American version, Potter was still hoping to shock and to deglamourise myths but he was dealing with all too familiar images and situations. What surprises, though, is that given the appropriate setting mistakes were made which gravely weaken the impact of the film.

An American director should have been able to guarantee the fine appropriateness of the musical routines but there is throughout an uncertainty of touch in this respect. Arthur's first "lip-sync"-ed song comes without warning and comes, as Paul Taylor points out, on a cut. It is sung by Elsie Carlisle and is totally disconcerting because as yet we have no idea who this character being played by a rather bemused Steve Martin actually is. Is he perhaps a castrato? Then the huge Busby Berkeley type routine that follows Arthur's visit to the bank comes far too early in the film and seems very overblown. Equally overblown and even ridiculous is the classroom routine that sees Eileen's charges transformed into a white tuxedo'd orchestra. And perhaps most jarringly of all we see Arthur and Eileen leave their cinema seats to become caught up in a Fred Astaire routine from *Follow the Fleet*; at this stage we are far too interested in the story in hand to be suddenly diverted by this very obvious and by now rather cliché'd reminder of the glamour that America could tantalisingly offer. Far more succesful are the scenes in which the music is used more intimately, when the "lip-sync"-ing is done within the sets of the main story rather than on a huge sound stage. The accordion man's *Pennies From Heaven*, sung in and outside a diner, is very moving (the actor is Vernel Bagneris, the singer Arthur Tracy). Christopher Walken has only one scene to establish his identity as a Chicago pimp but he takes the opportunity brilliantly as he dances, strips and seems to suggest everything that was thrilling and naughty in the city to the theme of Cole Porter's "Let's Misbehave".

As the film progresses so the power of the story takes over. The rather bland Steve Martin has to struggle to establish his identity and one certainly misses Bob Hoskins' genuinely proletarian earthiness, physically suggested frustration and ready wit. Jessica Harper as the wife is terrifyingly effective. The scene in which she reveals her scrawny, lipstick-painted breasts is as painful an intimate moment as one has seen on film and one well understands her desire to kill Arthur and her hope that 'they cut his thing off and bury it'. Just as disturbing is the way in which the Eileen of Bernadette Peters is transformed from a baby-doll schoolteacher to a woman who openly admits her sexual desire. The actress conveys the shock without ever really establishing a character. Arthur and Eileen's first copulation is as shocking here as the equivalent on the Gloucestershire floor but in the English version the actors effortlessly conveyed carnal desire whereas in the Illinois scene the actual sex seems quite out of character for both the timid teacher and the utterly romantic salesman. The fact that Arthur is a salesman, of course, places the character in what we might term the American cultural mainstream. 'Salesmen', according to this Arthur, 'have made America great'. In this context Potter does not need class to drive home his indictment: the Depression does the job of being the *deus ex machina* here. He does not need religion either, or rather the screenplay fails to drive home that point for in interviews Potter claimed that he had been successful in retaining that dimension. Here the accordion man is a very pathetic fool but his ragged rendering of "Rock Of Ages" lacks ironic overtones. We lose several layers of complication and inevitability but that does not particularly matter. The incredibly beautiful blind girl (played by Eliska Krupka) is rather regrettably made to smile as she takes her leave of Arthur. She has become Fate or perhaps a witch, but in general Potter is not in need of inexorable forces for in this American version of his story he has come to have a little more faith in his characters. We can see plainly that Eileen has 'burnt all her bridges' and by the end Steve Martin has won through to a performance that makes his comment 'I always knew something terrible was going to happen to me' all too appropriate. We have never had a sense of his Arthur struggling with as many conflicting urges as that of Bob Hoskins but what Steve Martin does give us is a very straightforward romantic optimist who made some foolish mistakes. On the gallows he "sings" the song "Pennies From Heaven" and the words and irony are as effective and as disturbing as at any point in the two tellings of the story. But there is a nagging thought. What one remembers above all from the television version is Bob Hoskins and the way that hope and frustration, pleasure and anxiety, break out in turn on that moon-like face. From the Hollywood version one remembers the two renderings of "Pennies From Heaven", one for the accordion man's great scene at the diner and the other at the gallows. Those moments, and perhaps the film, belong to Arthur Tracy singing Johnny Burke and Arthur Johnston's bitter-sweet poem; when the pennies are from heaven we are reminded to be sure that our 'umbrella is upside down'.

Potter at Large

Pennies From Heaven had been the turning point. "Dennis Potter" had erstwhile been a name, certainly one that was looked out for with keen anticipation and one that guaranteed challenging and conversation-provoking material, but just a name nonetheless. With hindsight we might conclude that little attention was given to the actual personality of that small group of pioneering television writers in the 1960s and 1970s so in any case there was little need to emphasise the particular reasons for Potter's low profile. Now all was changed and soon he was looming large in the national culture. His plays and adaptations were promoted as major television events and were shown at the National Film Theatre. His impact was no longer confined to the ghetto of television. He was writing movies for the big screen and in bookshops his novels were to be found alongside the texts of his most famous plays. And all the while we were learning more about the man. Arts reporting was a whole new fashion, something that was thought to sell newspapers and magazines; the age of the profile and in-depth interview had arrived and no subject was more popular than Potter. In the company of journalists and, increasingly, of radio reporters he would go over once again the main points in his career rewarding his more sympathetic interrogators with tantalising revelations or with a slightly fuller explanation of the extent to which he was a Christian, or a Marxist, or both. There was nearly always controversy, a feeling that with every play he had quite deliberately set out to breach the conventions of good taste that governed television. Nevertheless, for most of the 1980s, serious critics and "the chattering classes" greatly enjoyed his work and distanced themselves from the protests and discomfort of the stuffy suburbs and tabloid press. He had become a national institution, a guarantee that British television could be original and challenging. 'This has been the decade of Dennis Potter', explained the *Sunday Telegraph* in 1989, and this claim was buttressed by a quotation from the critic John Wyver to the effect that the man being profiled was 'unquestionably the most significant British television writer ever'.

Following *Pennies From Heaven* Potter's full measure of greatness as a television playwright was to be very evident in his single play *Blue Remembered Hills* which was broadcast in 1979 and then in the drama serial *The Singing Detective* which went out in 1986. It was these two works which above all pleased and satisfied his most genuine supporters and which guaranteed him an enormous fund of affection and expectation for the years ahead. Both productions were characterised by breathtaking innovatory techniques and yet so tight and effective was the writing and so smooth and professional the acting and direction that these never seemed anything other than entirely appropriate. These were ingenious plays but there was no hint of gimmickry. Both plays were historical; they dealt in various ways with the past and it was in this respect perhaps that the author was defining the constituency of his support. There was a real sense now that it was him as much as anyone who, even as he revolutionized the production techniques of television, was also ensuring that the medium remained faithful to, or was at least aware of, an older set of cultural values. They were both complex plays and there would have been as many different responses as there were viewers but certainly there were many for whom the satisfaction that Potter was now offering seemed a welcome relief from the new logic of the Thatcher era. The author himself was always to eschew and denounce nostalgia but he must surely have been aware of the way in which his best work (like so much of his conversation) seemed to stretch back in search of meaning and value into what was as much a collective as a personal memory. Clearly for Potter the past was not a pleasant or easy place but as he searched for his clues a vast audience was allowed to draw pleasure from the exercise as they lived once more through the cultural strands that had helped to define what they increasingly appreciated as having been a distinctive era in British history. Whatever the precise nature of his psychological insights it was the sheer familiarity and authenticity of the cultural context and idiom that earned affection for these two plays and which gave Potter a new, highly favoured status as television's star writer.

The very title of *Blue Remembered Hills* helped to establish its memorable qualities and the film ends with what was soon to become the distinctive voice of Potter himself ironically reciting what he was to refer to as A.E. Housman's 'aching little verse' from which the phrase was taken. What Potter has shown, of course, is that those fondly remembered shires were never innocent, that in their way they could be as deadly and as wounding as the wars which took so many young men away and made them nostalgic. The film does not have to rely entirely on Housman's verse to evoke the sense of Arcadia for the photography of Nat Crosby and his BBC crew had captured all the beauty and stillness of a long English summer day; the tragedy unfolds in the woods and meadows of a quintessentially English paradise. Of all Potter's television plays none was to transfer to the stage more successfully than this day in the life of seven schoolchildren and yet much is gained in the original by what we take initially to be a celebration of the countryside. The seven children wander aimlessly through this sylvan beauty filling their endless time with random speculation, idle boasts, half-hearted games, taunts that become increasingly pointed and an often vicious exploitation of the weaknesses of others; all the while alliances come and go, the degree of warmth and intimacy between various individuals fluctuates and there is a kaleidoscope of tears, laughter, intimacy and fear. The seven children were played by adults as Potter returned to the device he had first used in *Nigel Barton*. It takes just a second for that fact to sink in but from the outstart the actor Colin Welland, playing Willie, so successfully converts the author's full instructions into the mannerisms of a seven year old boy of the 1940s walking on his own that there is never any danger of the convention failing to work. Very soon we appreciate that the world of childhood is as full of cruelty, betrayal and pain as anything that will be experienced in later life, but we are left with the scary thought that perhaps these seven-year-olds have added an extra dimension of evil of which adults may not be capable. Not only do they lock the unfortunate Donald Duck in the burning barn until it is too late for him to escape but as the film ends the guilty six run away through the meadow all agreeing on, and obviously beginning to believe, the alibi that will establish their innocence: all the while they had been hiding in the woods.

There is more to this play, though, than this exploding of the myth of childhood innocence. The essential Potter dimension here is the way in which he shows his gang of seven imitating and feeding off the behaviour of adults, behaviour that they know so well from constant observation but which they do not fully comprehend. This is wartime and the boys play at soldiers, firing guns, throwing grenades and parachuting into the English countryside; meanwhile the girls with their dolls and prams play mothers and pick out the boys they would want to marry. There is always fierce competition between the boys and the war has introduced a new pecking order to this traditionally one-class community: 'Willie's Dad 'ent no blinking good for nothing at all — they oodn't even have him in the Army', whilst poor old Donald Duck's badly missed Dad is in the hands of the Japs so 'Him's as good as dead then — 'Xpect they'll tie him down on a great big hill of black ants. That's what the Japs do'. In the "Mothers and Fathers" games the children are all too well aware of the lines they have to speak: Angela is 'not slaving away here all day for him to come in at all hours and think his bit of tea have got to be ready and waiting', whilst the seven year old Donald knows exactly that in reply he has to say: 'Hurry up. I be off to the *bloody* pub in half a tick. To get *bloody* drunk'. Of course with Donald's Dad away the real mothers of the village have noted that his wife has been unfaithful and the hints and asides of the gossips have permeated down to the children. 'Our Mam', says John, 'says her's a bit of a thing — Our Mam said them bed sheets could tell a pretty tale'. 'Perhaps', sniggers Willie, 'her do wet the bed. Eh?' More frightening than anything in this play are the glimpses we have of the nastiness, bitterness and squalor of the proletarian adult world that surrounds these children and towards which they were heading. There were tears and evil deeds in the woods, but perhaps indeed the kids were better off there than anywhere else they were going to go. Those long summer days were as good as anything else was going to be.

DENNIS POTTER

In *The Singing Detective*, the work that was to be by far his most widely praised and appreciated, we are once again asked to remember the blue hills of childhood. Again the crucial pivotal moment takes place on a fine summer's day in the Forest of Dean of the early 1940s, and once more too we are concerned with the way in which a child sees and hears too much of the adult world for his own good. Potter's great gamble here was to construct a formidably complex time scale with the action taking place at four levels with several actors appearing in different guises. Over six episodes this complexity was too much for those devoted to naturalistic "soaps" but in essence the basic structure was simple. All the action takes place in the mind of Philip Marlow whom we first see in a hospital ward where he is being treated for an illness which has rendered him immobile and which has made his entire skin look 'as though boiling oil has been thrown over him' — 'he is cracked, scabbed, scaled, swollen, scarlet and snowy white, and boiling with pain'. Marlow, who is estranged from his wife Nicola, is the author of cheap detective thrillers written as parodies of the American 'Black Mask' genre. Through Marlow we relive the action of one of his books in which Marlow himself is 'the singing detective', a night-club singer hired to find out the identities of the mysterious men who are trying to kill Mark Binney in the dark dreary nights of 1945 London. Binney is caught up in some kind of espionage involving both Russians and former Nazis. We see him, too, in the company of women he meets in the nightclub; these are *femmes fatales*, prostitutes, spies and who knows what else? One of the girls he has known resembles Nicola and later we discover that the body in the Thames is indeed hers. Still later in the action we learn that the real life Marlow, as it were, the patient, has turned his out-of-print novel into a screenplay and he begins to realise that the sale of this to a production company might be his one chance of relieving his comparative destitution. As he talks to Nicola about this he begins to fantasise that she and her lover Finney (played by the same actor as Binney) are plotting to steal this script and pass it off as Finney's own work. All the while Marlow also relives his childhood in the Forest of Dean of the War Years. He recalls in particular the school bully Mark Binney whom he is forced into framing and betraying and also all the domestic squabbles which usually grew out of the tension between his mother from London and the Forest of Dean family she had married into and moved in with. The young Philip becomes aware that young couples get up to strange things in the woods and one day he sees Mark Binney's father making love to his own mother. Later his mother takes him away from the Forest and back to her own family in Hammersmith. 'When's our Dad going to come?' is young Philip's only concern and in his anxiety he develops his first psoriatic lesion and then lets out that he had seen her engaged in the scarcely comprehended activity of 'shagging' in the Forest. His mother is found dead in the Thames near Hammersmith Bridge, in the same spot where the fictional Nicola's body is to be found. The story of *The Singing Detective* is one in which, as Potter has explained, the writer Marlow deconstructs his life and comes to terms with the fact that it was Nicola he killed off in his book and that in childhood he betrayed another child in school and inadvertently revealed information that led to what might well have been his mother's suicide. As he relives and confronts his life his illness recedes and he is reconciled with Nicola.

We have again been given a classic Potter situation: a life has been scarred by an act of childhood betrayal and even more by an unwitting involvement in the sexual infidelity of the mother at the very point of marital breakdown and in a way that precipitates her suicide. Furthermore the central figure's own marriage which becomes the main focus of our attention has been destroyed by infidelity and in his own mind, at least, his wayward wife is driven to a similarly tragic end. The promiscuity of sexual betrayal is what poisons relationships and prevents any kind of emotional maturity and equilibrium. This is a gloomy and depressing scenario indeed but one which the playwright converts into a tremendously enjoyable piece of entertainment. There is no doubt that the success of this story was due to the deeply satisfying format. From the outset we are intrigued by the nature of Marlow's illness and disgruntlement and we are teased into fitting the various pieces of action together. The play itself becomes a thriller and we eagerly await further clues and the final explanation. But not only is Potter using the conventions of the most popular of all literary genres; he also totally submerges his play in the atmosphere of the Dashiell Hammett and Raymond Chandler world that this new Philip Marlow (not Marlowe as in Chandler) parodies in his fiction. The setting of Marlow's spy thriller in clubs and apartments along a night-time Thames has all the feel of one of Hammett's Sam Spade tales and certainly we are very much meant to be back in Hollywood's *film noir* version of *The Maltese Falcon*. The actual language, however, owes much more to Chandler and more than anything else it was to be Marlow's sardonic humour, one-liners and put-downs that fully justified his name and which accounted for the huge audience that his story attracted and held. In the real world of the 1980s the city had changed and so had the music and literature it inspired: essentially the city now belonged to the young; the middle-aged had retreated to the suburbs and there on Sunday evenings they were only too delighted to be taken back down those dark streets. The time was ripe for a Chandler-inspired knight-errant to put on his hat and turn up his collar as was indicated by so many contemporary advertisements and by such tributes to the Bogart era as the film *Dead Men Don't Wear Plaid*..

Potter had written a magnificently witty, crisp, snap-crackle-'n'-pop kind of dialogue that is funny on the page and quite unforgettable when delivered in Michael Gambon's plummy and yet silky lounge-lizard drawl. The scenes in which Marlow fends off Potter's latest antagonist in a white coat, Dr Gibbon, are the most humorous he has ever written. Unlike most of the playwright's medical experts at least this one is on the right track but that only stirs Marlow into further defensive evasiveness and into the smoke-screen of word games. All of this is authentically Chandleresque. Marlow tells Dr Gibbon that as a psychiatrist he should go to football games 'because that's where all the nutters are nowadays. On the terraces. Except at Fulham — That's where you go to be alone'. The Doc is teased about his slowness in catching a reference, for Marlow had him 'down for a man who could strike matches on his thumbnail'. Marlow (and Potter) is careful to cover himself and at one point he talks to Finney of his 'unhelpful, paperback-soiled, mid-Atlantic, little side-of-the-mouth quips' but most viewers will disregard this particular piece of self-denigration as they wait for the next put-down. 'Do you know how many O-levels you have to fail to be a nurse?', Marlow asks the ward. truggling to suppress an erection as a beautiful nurse tends to his body he thinks of all the most boring things and of course a

Welsh male voice choir comes to mind. His Indian neighbour offers a sweet but Marlow quips that 'sour' is more his line. The whole play is about the vulnerability of Marlow: we see him as a child pathetically turning to God in prayer and we know that he has had direct experience of the bogey man in the form of a half-human scarecrow who merges into a memory of a bullying schoolteacher precisely at the moment of his parents' separation. And yet what lingers is the arrogant bombast and wit of the adult Marlow as he surveys the mediocrity that he sees from his hospitable bed. His fictional detective is a perfect *alter ego* and the cocky, irritating certainty of Gambon's effortlessly superior 'Am I right or am I right?' is the lasting memory of the play.

Potter's evocation of the 1940s is completed by the extensive use of the period's popular music. It is the strains of "I've Got You Under My Skin" that initially link the fictional night club with the hospital ward where Marlow is suffering from psoriasis. Soon thereafter it is the marvellous spectacle of a medical team suddenly breaking into "Dry Bones" which effectively clinches Marlow's distancing himself from the crazy world that surrounds him and ensures that we see things from his perspective rather than that of the system. The authorities question his attitude towards his illness but what is important to him is their attitude. In the rest of the play the music is used in a very specific and ingenious way to bind together the various levels of the action. Marlow's fictional detective is a singing detective who can introduce each episode of his own adventure with an appropriately ironic song performed on the nightclub stage because, in his own memory, each moment in his mother's path to the tragedy at Hammersmith was associated with a particular tune, one heard either on the radio that was a constant background to every family scene or one performed by his parents themselves at the workingmen's club. All the different Marlows, Philip and the others, are bound into the one thought process by the tunes and the sexual relationships and juxtapositions can be defined exactly. This occurs most memorably when the Inkspots version of "Do I Worry?" accompanies the scene at the workingmen's club when Raymond Binney gently touches Mrs Marlow; her husband notices and what Philip has seen in the woods is confirmed. We, the audience, are prepared now for the separation of his parents. The use of the music, then, is fully justified both in terms of the play's construction and its psychology. In his best known comment on this subject Potter explained that the songs were like 'stones thrown' at the bed-ridden Marlow from out of his past; they were the sharpest and most painful reminder of all the bad moments that had contributed to his wreckage. That much is clear and acceptable but there does remain an element of ambiguity, for the songs, like the singing detective and the novel he inhabits, are all very much associated with the rarefied, artificial, commercial and rather sinister atmosphere of the Skinscope nightclub. The music is used by Potter to bind all the action together and yet within the telling of the tale it is unmistakeably attributed to the nightlife ghetto. Like the detective idiom it belongs to a showbiz genre, a world of cheap, easy stereotypes. 'You and your songs', taunts Nicola. 'Yeh', confesses Marlow, 'Banality with a beat'.

Marlow's self-denigration and defensiveness are entirely in character but they are also a reflection of Potter's own attitude. In what he has said about this play Potter always emphasises the banality and triviality of the music, implies resentment at the nostalgia that is induced and even at one point talked of how he hated the songs. And yet he is unable and unwilling to do without their power or deny the associations. At one stage he talked of 'the faint ache' which 'is usually dismissed as one of the more cheap and useless form of nostalgia' but then conceded that 'the singing detective knows they can do more than this.' Here again he is rather wanting things both ways and, as was the case with *Pennies From Heaven*, he is not fully prepared to accept the music on its own terms. He had wanted to blame the music for Arthur's lack of realism without realising the extent to which it had helped to confirm so many of his positive attributes. Similarly he wants us to appreciate Marlow's sense that the music is banal even as we are overwhelmed by its role in his thought process. Of course viewers loved *The Singing Detective* because of the music and of course the soundtrack was soon available commercially. On the sleeve both Potter and his producer, Kenith Trodd, explained the dramatic use of the music but only in printing that was small enough for most people to ignore as they just sat back and enjoyed Bing Crosby, Dick Haynes and Ella Fitzgerald. These tunes will mean different things to different people but one suspects that enthusiasts will never have to apologise for playing them or feel ashamed of any effect or association they may have. Surely we all know that Cole Porter, Hoagy Carmichael and Johnny Mercer were accomplished and clever poets and accurate observers who were lucky enough to work with very talented musicians, and it was a case of "what oft was thought" ne'er so well being expressed or delivered. There is no reason why a nightclub singer performing "I Get Along Without You Very Well" needs to be explained or excused any more than a detective commenting on the fickleness of women or an author in a hospital bed struggling to achieve happiness. In *The Singing Detective* Potter's use of the music is never anything less than effective, legitimate and intelligent and yet one senses, both from the use of the popular culture idiom and his subsequent comments, that he is just a little ashamed of the music's power and he distances himself from it. Meanwhile, of course, all the charm and magic of the music accrues to his script. He is equally ashamed of nostalgia but one suspects he is fully aware of quite why this play was so popular. Potter's Marlow is a marvellous creation especially as realised by Michael Gambon; what better compère could there be to invite us back into that favourite dance-band era? And on the sleeve Potter gives the game away by signing off with 'Then play them again ... Sam'.

Dr Gibbon knows from the start what Marlow's trouble is. He tells him quite bluntly 'You don't like women. Do you?' and pointedly quotes from his patient's detective novel the passage in which 'the sweaty farce' of sex is summed up: 'Mouth sucking wet — limb thrashing upon limb — organs spurt out smelly stains and sticky betrayals'. The experiences of weakness and betrayal have alienated Marlow from the act of sex and made it impossible for him to sustain a normal adult relationship. Somehow his terrible infliction is a manifestation of his sexual disgust and we see that subside as the doctors and Nicola force him through a confrontation with what he has suppressed and into a new wholeness. The healing of Marlow is a fascinating enough process and is guaranteed to hold audiences but there is no denying that the unpleasant, unwholesome pill of this play's psychological truth is quite considerably coated with the sugar of Potter's wit, the dance-band music, the Chandleresque idiom and Gambon's mellifluous throw-away diction. It is this coating which makes *The Singing*

Dectective into Potter's most successful and genuinely liked work; the atmosphere, the mythology and the wit were all running together. By the same token it can be argued that as Potter has stuck with his same theme, that of the anxiety, unhappiness, inadequacy and violence generated by memories of sexual betrayal or exploitation, so the success of any particular treatment of this theme will be determined by the extent to which the psychological truths are coated or mythologised. Nothing that he has done since 1986 has been so admired or enthused over as the tale of Philip Marlow, and critics and audiences have often been alienated by the absence of a comforting mythology or idiom or by the excessive hatred and violence emerging out of the sexual chemistry. The skills of the superbly professional and experienced writer inject wit, intriguing ironies and the comforting satisfaction of genre into everything he does but there has been a cruelty, a brutality, a determination to take everything through to an ultimately bloody conclusion and, it will be said, a reductionism that many of his supporters have found frustrating.

A more pleasing and more palatable Potter was to been seen in *Dreamchild*, the 1985 movie version of the play *Alice* that he had written in 1965. As with *Where Adam Stood* it is difficult not to avoid the conclusion that the author has benefited from the restraint imposed by historical circumstances however free the adaptation and original the script. There are moments when one wonders whether Potter is going to unleash a damnation of American commercialism but here the New York of the 1930s is depicted quite favourably and the entertainers that Alice Liddell encounters, whether they be broadcasters or musicians, are seen to be trying to enchant in almost the same way as the storytelling "Lewis Carroll" of her Victorian childhood. In the key moment of the film the full choir and orchestra of Columbia University perform the Mock Turtle's song and Alice recalls the Reverend Charles Dodgson's rendering of it by the river in Oxford: she and her sister had giggled, he was overwhelmed with embarrassment and stuttered to a halt; only after a while had she given him a kiss of reconciliation. The elderly Alice explains to her companion that 'love is an emotion that always frightens me and yet I can recognise it when I see it'. So brilliant is Ian Holm's performance as Dodgson that we fully realise the truth of that remark. The very beautiful young Alice (played by Amelia Shankley) had reason to be frightened. She was quite clearly loved and in that moment by the Thames, as "Will You, Won't You Join the Dance" was sung by Dodgson, was guilty of a betrayal that she would never forget. This is as moving as any moment in Potter and as one cherishes this film it is worth making the contrast with his next feature film, *Track 29*, released in 1987.

This was a rewrite by Potter of his 1974 play *Schmoedipus* in which a suburban housewife encounters a young man claiming to be her long-lost son, the young illegitimate child immediately taken away from her after she had given birth aged fifteen. The young man metamorphoses into the father of the child and then again becomes her lover as we realise that he is a figment of her imagination expressing all her desires, not least the realisation that she must kill her husband. The most effective feature of the film is the depiction, often in comic terms, of the utter sterility, in both senses, of this suburban marriage in which differing sexual memories have led to differing emotional and sexual needs; she wants affection from "Daddykins" and a child, he wants to play with his trains and has learnt the bitter lesson that 'trains and women don't mix'. Both Teresa Russell as the wife and Gary Oldman as her alleged son are brilliantly cast, both have the troubling sexuality of child-adults, but their scenes are embarrassing and one becomes all too aware of the sheer confusion and intrusion of the allegory. Both actors, as well as the general themes of 'the dirty little secret' and of childhood being 'as good as occupation as any', would have been better served by the naturalism and poetic symbolism of Tennessee Williams. Moreover the production team have been seduced by the conventions of the big screen into overstatement. The husband (Christopher Lloyd) is not left in the position of being a boring model train enthusiast for he turns a rally of loco enthusiasts into a political convention or even an evangelical meeting as he gives vent to all the ambition and sexual drive of an Elmer Gantry. Regrettably he hijacks that wonderful song "Chattanooga Choo Choo" in the process. Worst of all, however, his death, whether symbolic or no, whether in his wife's mind or no, is all too graphically and horrifyingly depicted as the naked child-lover of her thoughts leaps out of a cupboard and stabs him repeatedly, all the while clinging to his body in a parody of sex. The Oedipal and Freudian structure of the tale is pretty basic and crude but it is the hopelessly fashionable attempt at a comic-book, special-effects movie that disturbs. It is not only the house itself which feels as if it were left over from the latest version of *The Exorcist*.

One sensed at this time that Potter was looking for the ideal milieu in which to set his stories of emotional disturbance and sexual anxiety. His best bet was surely the one he had utilised in his first and only play written specifically for the stage, *Sufficient Carbohydrate*, which was first performed in 1983. The story concerns five people (two couples and the son of one of the husbands by his first marriage) who are vacationing in a villa on a Greek island. The group dynamics constitute the action of the play but in truth we are really only interested in one character and what the audiences were confronted with was in essence the kind of dramatic monologue that had dominated the plays of John Osborne. We are asked to consider the experiences of a middle-aged Englishman, Jack Barker, the son of a vicar and until recently the head of of a Norfolk food manufacturing company which has been bought out by an American giant for whom he has to work. The American company is headed by Eddie Vosper, a go-getting philistine who is having an affair with Jack's wife. On the island Jack drinks himself into oblivion, hitting and kicking Eddie's new wife as he does so, and the only relieving comfort is that the old black freighter, which he sees cross the horizon every morning and which becomes the symbol of his idealism, his romanticism and of all his good feelings, is at least something that Eddie's son Clayton can see as well. Perhaps the steamer does not exist at all, perhaps all the action of the play has been imagined, but at least in stark contrast to the bearpit of the adult world there is Clayton's sensitivity to remind Jack of everything he once treasured.

Possibly too much rests on that black freighter which has clear origins in the work of Eugene O'Neill and Tennessee Williams but this is a strikingly effective play which has been generally overlooked since it was disappointingly filmed (as *The Visitors*) in 1987. The fact that the Vospers are American highlights Jack's Englishness and it is particularly the virtues of an English childhood that he wants to recall, a time when with God caring for the world 'Everything Was All Right', everything was 'filled to the brim with fear and wonder'. Jack's tragedy is that half of him is 'still that child', hence his love of Keats and his response to the Aegean in Keatsian terms; it is the romantic past in him that sees the freighter. But his other half has been shaped by the necessity of dealing with adults who 'eat people' and who have 'blood on their teeth', whether they be executives with dubious ethics or deceiving wives. We are invited to share Jack's disgust and sadness but at the same time we warm to him because of his savage wit which has become his main line of defence. He is a pathetic drunken old sod but (especially as played with relish by Dinsdale Lansden in the West End) he takes the other characters to the cleaners. When he reports that 'Something very nasty crawled into my mouth', Mrs Vosper's reply is 'That's strange! Something very nasty usually crawls *out*'. But we love every word of it especially, of course, when he's slagging the Americans. And this is not just grandstanding or virtuoso wit and anger for its own sake for, all the while, our sense of his 'sour, tired disappointment' is deepened.

Potter stayed very much in that milieu for his 1986 novel *Ticket to Ride* which was filmed in 1992 as *Secret Friends*. The novel is an intriguing psychological thriller which rests on the tension between a man's wife and home in the West of England and the sex commercially available in London, the two locales being linked by a series of train journeys which we pick up in no particular sequence. We return here to an earlier theme of Potter's, that of the prostitute and the wife being interchangeable, and the tension of the piece rests on speculation as to whether the central character John has killed his wife or a prostitute although there is always the possibility that we have just had glimpses into the private workings of his mind. The John Buck of this story is clearly of the same ilk as Jack Barker; he is a commercial artist who has lost his job with an advertising agency; he too is a vicar's son, the product of a puritanical and authoritarian manse and his bleak life there was only made bearable by the creation of a wicked *alter ego* who can shout the forbidden "Bugger!" and think evil thoughts. The adult John's trouble, as his wife Helen explains, is that sex for him is dirty and can therefore only be satisfactory if it is imagined as illicit and commercial. This is an interesting enough dilemma but what sustains the interest is the way in which it is worked out within the two locales: the visiting businessman's view of the prostitutes' domain that is Paddington is brilliantly evoked and is then contrasted with that oh-so-lovely English village where we find, in fact, that his wife could well have been a call-girl before their marriage and that the best friends who visit, Angela and Martin, have been the lovers of John and Helen respectively. At what appears to be the ideal English home John's notion of sex as a dirty commodity has been confirmed, not banished. In the 1992 film version some of the power of the story is lost by a dependence on overstated class stereotypes and by an unthinking and unnecessary exploitation of Gina Bellman's beauty as Helen but the suggestion of sexual infidelity as the snake in the bourgeois grass is brilliantly conveyed, not least in a memorable dinner party scene of knowing looks and innuendo. This surely must now be Potter's world.

Hard on the heels of *Ticket to Ride* came another novel *Blackeyes* in which our attention is again directed towards the "nouveau affluent" in Southern England. This time we are introduced to the customs and practices of that vastly profitable and hugely influential coming together of advertising agencies and magazine publishers and to the way in which they had created a London in their own image. The novel is unsatisfactory in many ways and the fact that Dennis Potter opted to direct the television film of *Blackeyes* that followed is surely the main explanation of why those unsatisfactory features not only remained but were exacerbated. As with *The Singing Detective* and *Ticket to Ride* the story is told at several levels and out of sequence. Again we are meant to be satisfied by the process of fitting pieces together and the unravelling of clues. This time, however, the author's cleverness is far too infuriating and as new perspectives and levels of objective reality emerge one just feels cheated. We have been invited to care but then learn it is all a game. That is bad enough but the real problem with *Blackeyes* is the author's mixed feelings about the milieu portrayed and the central characters involved. For all the scathing denunciation of the advertising world, the book and the film have all the feel of having been made from the inside and of being not entirely displeased with the prospect of long lunches of salmon and dry white wine. For much of the time we are invited to base our judgement on the experience of the model Blackeyes who is made to accept her status as a sex symbol, who will sell any commodity she is asked to promote and who finds no pleasure or meaning in the casual sex that goes with the territory. Far from extending any sympathy, however, we just respond to her as the masturbatory fantasy and disposable image that she never ceases to be. She is the definition or depiction of a thing, a neutral object, a doll, in no sense a character and in no sense an invitation to a critique. We are no more surprised to find her here than we are when we come across a nude pin-up in *Playboy*.

At first our attention is caught by Blackeyes herself but we soon lose interest in her because she is not going to develop. The main tension of the story is that between the ageing author Maurice (James Kingsley) and his niece Jessica. The ugly secret which we have to fight our way towards is that many years ago the young Jessica was encouraged to masturbate her uncle as they were returning in his car from a day's excursion to the park. After a long fallow period as a writer Kingsley resurrects his reputation by a novel, the story of Blackeyes, which is largely based on Jessica's recollections of her own career as a model. The story, then, is of how Jessica seeks her revenge, first for her abuse and then for the plagiarism. She is made eventually to kill her uncle, but the trouble for the reader is in our having to use this word 'made', for ultimately Jessica is as much a device and non-person as her fictional *alter ego* Blackeyes. Another author, another voice, perhaps that of the man named on the cover (and certainly Potter himself narrates the film version), steps in to explain that Jessica was not intelligent enough to rewrite the story of Blackeyes so as to rescue it from the suicide that Kingsley had prescribed. Potter is playing a game as he makes the point that the male author is always God and is ultimately responsible for every aspect of his characters so if he wants to patronise his own creations and deny women heroic status he can do it. This final denial of Jessica's independence and reality is meant to clinch our appreciation of the closed totality of male dominance with respect to how women are seen but in practice it just deeply offends, all the more so as the memory of Maurice James Kingsley will linger on. When we first learn of his offence we should be demanding his imprisonment and then when Jessica kills him we should be cheering loudly. Instead of that we will recall him quite fondly — a bit of a dirty old bugger who should never have done that to his niece but what a great English character! He stinks, he lives in a seedy apartment with his beloved teddy and he is a fraudulent opportunist, but if this is what the world of English letters has come to so be it, for we can still cherish his mastery of the classics. He has a quote for every occasion and we warm to the cavalier way he dismisses everything that is second-rate and spurious in contemporary criticism and journalism. Potter has done his job too well with Kingsley for rather than summing up the shabby hypocrisy and decadence of what passes for literary fame in the metropolis he has created a memorable "old devil" whose further adventures we would rather follow. Jessica's whole existence then was in vain, her every effort futile. Of course that was Potter's aim and to achieve it he took many risks, the backfiring of which he should have anticipated. The fleshing out of the characters in British television's full-blooded and utterly professional way just made matters worse.

So much had Potter become a sharp and witty observer of the contemporary chattering classes that it was something of a surprise that for his latest television mini-series he returned to more distant autobiographical themes. In truth it felt a little as if, having used the music of the thirties in *Pennies From Heaven* and of the forties in *The Singing Detective*, he was more or less obliged to come up with an idea for the 1950s; and what was more obvious than his own experience of National Service, a subject he had dealt with in his earlier play *Lay Down Your Arms*? In the outcome, *Lipstick on Your Collar*, the basic material was very familiar. At least *Lay Down Your Arms* had been a single play but now a fairly simple and undeveloped story is stretched somewhat thinly over six episodes. The general denunciation of the upper-class twits who run the War Office at the time of Suez rests pretty much on crude stereotypes and this all seems rather old hat. Undoubtedly the main problem of the play is the split focus as we follow the story of two very different young men who represent various aspects of late adolescence. Private Francis Francis (Giles Thomas) is an irritating provincial square with a maddening Welsh accent, and though he naively flirts with danger and encounters religious fanaticism in his own family we know that his love of Pushkin and Chekhov will see him through to safety. Far more interesting and attractive is the city slicker Private Hopper (Ewan McGregor) and one should really have been asked to follow his story, for all the rock and roll and ballads played are his music and a reflection of his energies. Of course the fact that the sexuality and restlessness of an Elvis Presley were setting up vibrations in London, and even in Whitehall, at the time of Suez is largely a matter of juxtapositioning rather than the basis of a political critique and this is only one possible way in which differences of class and of attitudes towards Empire have been investigated. The best thing in the play is Louise Germaine's portrayal of the "dumb blonde" Sylvia, and here again one suspects that the author might not have fully realised how memorable was to be the character he had created, for she is far more interesting and worthy of our attention than the two male heroes who compete for her. She is a genuine urban type, the working-class chiseller who is going to have to survive using only her beauty and her realism. Every indignity is imposed on her; she lives in a dingy flat, her husband abuses her, hits her and makes love to her violently. She sells herself to a dirty old man and then, at the very moment she spies a romantic escape route in the shape of Francis, her husband is killed in a gruesome accident and then buried by a priest who cannot remember the deceased's name. Throughout, her look and her language are directly to the point and she retains her dignity and her independence come what may. Straight from her husband's interment she is back in her kitchen being screwed by Hopper. These two Londoners really do deserve each other and the freedom to enjoy each other and their music. Who really cares about Suez? As Sylvia says: 'You gotta live, haven't yuh!'

* * *

The publicity given to *Lipstick on Your Collar* and to its author made the need for an assessment very apparent. As the sheer volume and regularity of Potter's literary output continued to impress and demand analysis so the man increasingly stepped forward to be interviewed and to provide a full commentary that needed to be set alongside his fictions. During the course of the 1980s he surrendered what had been his hitherto relative anonymity and became a far more identifiable figure, and one consequence was a buttressing of the notion of him as a highly distinctive author. Throughout this volume Potter has been discussed purely as an "auteur", as if he were as much the sole progenitor of his films and plays as he clearly is of his published texts. Of course the reality had been that, for all the quality of his texts and the fullness of his instructions, producers, directors, cameramen, designers, composers, arrangers and not least actors had themselves contributed as auteurs to the final product that was almost exclusively associated with the Potter name. We have noticed how Bob Hoskins, Michael Gambon, Ian Holm and Colin Welland had made the texts effective and even added depths and shades of meaning of their own. Obviously it is more difficult to assess precisely what was contributed by directors like Gareth Davies, Lionel Harris, Piers Haggard and Jon Amiel, cameramen like Nat Crosby and designers like Tim Harvey and Bruce Macadie, let alone the even less often listed personnel in charge of editing and arranging the vital musical score. What could be identified was the increasingly clear preference on Potter's part to be even more in charge of his own work, to be even more fully the sole auteur.

The press followed with growing interest the story (and it is obviously one that needs one day to be told in full) of how the increasingly successful playwright fell out with the BBC, had a difference of opinion with London Weekend Television and even broke with his long time champion collaborator and producer Kenith Trodd whom he had known since National Service days. The rise of independent film-making was obviously a godsend for Potter and his associates as has been the opening up of the international television market: *The Singing Detective*, for example, was made in association with the Australian Broadcasting Corporation. The new dispensation finally allowed the writer to be his own director but with results that were not satisfying. Potter is far from unique in that respect and one thinks of the many American film auteurs (Francis Ford Coppola and Michael Cimino most readily come to mind) who bucked the production system in search of greater freedoms but who in the absence of creative team work rather lost their edge. What has been most worrying in Potter's recent work is a reliance on class and sex stereotypes, the failure to establish the focus of experience and core of reality and, above all perhaps, an uncertainty with regard to format. The six part mini-series obviously recommends itself both to the television companies and the production team but what was so right for *Pennies From Heaven* and *The Singing Detective* has been inappropriate on subsequent occasions. One longs now for the mastery of those single plays like *Blue Remembered Hills* and perhaps Potter would do well to bear in mind the brilliantly successful formats worked so well in their different ways by Woody Allen in New York and Alan Ayckbourn in Scarborough. The true auteur, whether in film or the theatre, can do much with repertory companies which have regular access to a wider market for single works.

Perhaps it is only critics and people in the trade who are interested in Potter's commercial arrangements and in the credits that flash past at the end of a transmission. There has been far more interest, though, in the way in which the writer has begun to explain himself, to tell, in the first instance, the story of his painful and unsightly indisposition, of how drugs brought relief and then allowed releases in which he could travel and become far more heavily involved in the production process, even if there were frequent periods of relapse and unpleasant side effects. Quite obviously it was *The Singing Detective* which dramatically encouraged critics and columnists alike to focus on his own illness and to pick up on the clear implication of that play that the illness from which both Potter and Marlow had suffered was in some way psychosomatic. As journalists met with the writer, and of course these meetings usually took place at times of remission, they could not help but notice the deformity of his hands and so they were prompted into purple passages of analysis as to how illness and the intensity demanded by creativity were related. But even more, of course, they were tempted to speculate about the degree of autobiography in the plays under consideration and in this they were given every encouragement. Potter talked generally about his background and his illness but there could also be references to more specific events.

The sexual abuse of a young boy was an element in his 1969 play *Moonlight on the Highway* and then, in the 1973 novel *Hide and Seek*, a decisive event in the psychological state being examined was the way in which 'Forest boy, like Forest girl — found out — about the predatory appetites of the fully grown'. Then in his introduction to *Waiting for the Boat*, published in 1984, Potter spoke directly of 'something foul and terrible that happened to me when I was ten years old' when he had been 'caught by an adult's appetite and abused out of innocence'. In 1989 Potter refused to go on when the *Sunday Telegraph* Profile writer asked whether he had been abused by a male relative, but in 1992 Ginny Dougary of *The Times* learnt that this indeed had been the case: 'It was the drink, you know, and it didn't happen all that often'. In other interviews he has given ample indication that at this stage he wants to go no further and surely everyone respects his right to release private information of this sort only when he feels the need. What he has done, though, is to say enough to show that the emphasis on sexual abuse, guilt and anxiety in his work is rooted in his own experience and must be taken as serious commentary on issues and phenomena that for decades society as a whole chose to ignore. All too often interrogators can be seen wanting Potter to confirm autobiography in his work and they obviously sense that they are being teased, whereas an intelligent critic ought readily to accept both the author's right to establish the limits of his privacy and the distinction made between memory and fiction. Like all writers Potter is not writing of his experiences but rather out of them. Clearly he has preoccupations, preoccupations which will not interest many people and which have positively alienated many others. Even Kenith Trodd concedes that Potter is 'sexually preoccupied' and for the critic Brian Robertson his whole outlook in that respect is essentially 'adolescent'. But Potter will not go away; his work keeps on appearing, finds backers and then attracts audiences. His sheer professionalism has much to do with this. The story will be well told, there will be much to talk about and of course there will be shocks and surprises and something not seen on television before. Potter the showman will have done his job. But more than that, any new Potter play will be challenging and rewarding because of the way in which his own preoccupations, however extreme and overstated, will have been incorporated into a story that will nag away at half-suppressed memories, anxieties and guilt in the minds of his audience. Not everyone in the audience will have been sexually abused at the age of ten (although in the 1990s we know that the statistics in that respect would be much higher than had hitherto been suspected) but that audience will be large and loyal precisely because the honesty and darkness of the author's theme will ask questions of the culture that are rarely put.

It is undeniable that it was just straightforward nostalgia that allowed Potter to gain his largest audiences. It is equally clear that nostalgia is not really his aim. But he is a writer who comes to us from the past and who quite deliberately assesses the present and the process of change from the perspective of the Forest of Dean in the 1940s. He grew up in the context of shared beds and bedrooms, of outside toilets and of baths taken in front of the whole family. He has lived on into an age of suburban affluence in which so many of the basic aspects of everyday life can be magically disguised or forgotten. In a very fundamental way Potter is simply the man who reminds the newly affluent not only of the world of which they or their parents were products but also of the fact that the sights, sounds, smells and desires which had once seemed so obvious and immediate have not really left us and that instincts and needs do not change in the suburbs. He remains by instinct a peasant or a proletarian not because he admires or romanticizes that world — obviously there could be little danger of that — but because he recalls all too vividly the ways in which purely physical instincts would be expressed directly. In those miners' cottages, and even in those woods, there was nowhere to hide. Affluence was to allow too many to hide.

The writer himself, of course, achieved affluence and very clearly his attitude towards it has always been ambivalent. There is every reason to believe that he has enjoyed the comforts that his hard-earned wealth has allowed — his home, visits to London and the States, good food and good wine. Yet those things are never celebrated in his work. What we could take to be the fruits of a career, the benefits that accrue to the talented and successful, are always depicted in his work as the very circumstances in which betrayal, anger and abuse are likely to occur. Potter's own experience of a transition from worker's cottage to affluence was not an uncommon one in that unprecedently affluent era that followed the Second World War and one should not underestimate the extent to which his investigations of the resonances of that age of social transformation has accounted for his place in the cultural history of our time. For many people the steps towards maturity and success in this period were not taken without difficulty. Few, it was true, were to experience the extreme traumas of Potter which had included a public betrayal of his parents and the sudden onset of a debilitating illness at the very point at which the world seemed to be his oyster, but there were countless viewers who could respond to Potter's emphasis on those many crises that occur as family, class and sexual loyalties have to be defined even as there is pressure from new opportunities. Perhaps there were many too who appreciated his oft repeated dramatic promise that men and women who entered the promised land of suburban affluence did so carrying scars and wounds consequent upon the inevitable rejection of parental and class ties and having to discipline a sexuality that had already been sullied by the passion of others in childhood and then by one's own passions as casual and commercial sex had become available. Everyone took their own case histories into the suburbs and not everyone could now exercise the discretion and the control that sustained intimacy required. However neat the privet hedge, however white the carpet and light and airy the rooms, the stains of guilt and the impulse to anger will surface to taint what can only be a camouflage.

Throughout this whole exercise of relating the burdens of one's psychological past to the process of social change Potter has always displayed a thoroughly ambivalent attitude towards popular culture and indeed he fully admits to having problems with the whole phenomenon. We saw that the most obvious feature of his own socialism and of his deep commitment to an egalitarian democracy was his belief in a common culture and yet he has always found it difficult fully to associate himself with the common culture that has developed in his own era. Nowhere has he defined at length the common culture that he would regard as ideal but one can readily sense what he is getting at. He has always spoken openly of his English patriotism even as he denies that his patriotism has any connection with that of the country's social élite as expressed all too vocally by the Tories. His patriotism is that of the common man and is associated above all with the kind of Englishness that was learnt in elementary and secondary schools. It is to do with a love of language and verse and the kind of Protestant directness and honesty thought characteristic of Shakespeare, Hazlitt, Dickens and Orwell. That was indeed a mental and emotional framework into which several generations of Brtish schoolchildren were inducted and one deeply regrets its passing. Yet Potter can never concede that this alone could not have been the sole basis of a modern urban culture. Life in an industrial society would have stayed bleak indeed had it not been for a commercial entertainment industry and the electronic equipment it rapidly devised. Potter himself would have emerged as the first to be dissatisfied with village hall and village green homespun entertainment and yet from the start he was always to distrust the sugary sweetness of broadcast music and the stridency of the jukebox. Even more there was a deep suspicion of those outsiders, those showmen, those word- and tune-smiths (Jewish and wearing eye-shades, as perceived by the salesmen in *Pennies From Heaven*) in London, New York and Hollywood who were selling what has now become the new culture as if it were any old commodity.

It was of course Potter's own sensitivity that made him so angry about popular culture. Things that he wanted to be precious and holy were being bandied about in the market place, things that he found so difficult and so intimate were dismissed or resolved so easily. And yet all the while the undoubted power of the words and music were there and could hardly be avoided. Perhaps the greatest irony of his whole career is that the two plays in which he above all else sought to indict popular music became his most successful plays, not least because of the music which itself was given a new lease of life. The music of the 1930s is condemned for seducing Arthur Parker into illicit love and irresponsibility and that of the 1940s is used to sustain the way in which Marlow is tortured by his past, and yet for audiences the marvellous music will be appreciated afresh for its own sake and if anything be enhanced by being associated not with the weakness of Arthur but rather with his admirable ambition and optimism and not with Marlow's illness but with his urbanity and wit. In fact Potter's own popularity was greatly boosted precisely because he was now commonly associated with the nostalgia for dance band music and was thought of as being particularly sensitive to it. Of course, only Potter knows what the music actually means in his own life for clearly one of the characteristics of the radio era was that certain tunes could become very personal, could be particularly associated with moments of sadness or unhappiness, with the words of a song seeming to be either very relevant or of course totally inappropriate. But surely it was far more general for those who had an ear for this music to respond to it positively? Perhaps it was the case that the Depression of the 1930s created a new vogue for simple straightforward philosophies about what was important in life but it was also a time when the masses were fascinated by the possibility of improvement and much popular culture was associated with a new urban style that was thought of as sophisticated. The radio, gramophone and cinema gave ordinary folks everywhere instant access to a more glamorous world, a world that some took to be illusory whilst others set off in search of it. Mostly, though, it was just accepted as being highly attractive and offering good value entertainment. The music and films were shot through with irony — the songwriters and producers knew that, as did their audiences; there was a bitter-sweet quality to most entertainment and that too was widely appreciated but, above all, in the classic era of the thirties and forties popular culture was gratefully accepted as an antidote to a drab reality and one which allowed a celebration of some of the better things of life.

In a discussion of an era that he defines as one when 'America dreamed of itself as a singing fairy tale for grown ups, with a happy ending' Stephen Holden argues that the songs were 'more than just pop confections' for 'they added up to a kind of secular catechism that sweetly but firmly instructed people on the rules of behaviour in a world where America knew best and good triumphed over evil'. The implication here that popular music was in a sense a substitute for religion is one that has been commonly made. We can see now that the churches were quite right to be frightened of so much popular culture as they saw young people defect to the radio and the movies. But of course Holden is implying too that the new 'catechism' taught restraint and discipline and indicated limits as much as the old, and it was only in later decades that entertainment urged indulgence, promiscuity and the doing of one's own thing. To an almost unique degree it is Dennis Potter who has bracketed the popular religion and popular culture of the 1930s but he has done so in a far more specific way than most commentators on the history of entertainment. Catchy tunes were common to both, and Potter has always stressed the relevance of Noel Coward's famous remark about the 'extraordinary potency of cheap music' to both the revivalist meeting and showbiz. What makes Potter so interesting is that he also listened to the words. He has described how Sunday after Sunday he listened to the promises and summonses to action in the hymns of Ira Sankey, only later realising that so much of this was empty bombast. All the great metaphors and the splendid rhetoric carefully avoided the subject of Death and indeed they seemed increasingly irrelevant to most immediate aspects of life. So Potter ended up blaming Sankey and perhaps religion as a whole 'for the crucial first few inches of the gap' which had 'opened up between every single one of my early dreams and every single part of my earliest realities'. This substantially has remained the case against both the preachers and the showmen; they seduced by means of their sweet tunes and words and yet they could not deliver. It might be argued by some that we have evidence here of Potter's essential immaturity for surely the ability to cope with that graduation from fairy-tale to reality is the test of adulthood; we accept that there is no Father Christmas and get on with the job of building more substantial relationships. Was Potter just someone who took all the metaphors of childhood too lite-rally? Did he really have to listen to every word and dwell on every promise?

Well, perhaps he did. We have arrived really at the litmus test of whether one values his work or no. The detractors will dismiss much of it as adolescent whereas his admirers will point to that all-pervading quality of childlike disappointment which marks so many of his plays. The latter might well appreciate, too, that there were probably very specific events both in his childhood and adult life which have helped to substain both an interest in promises made and in the disappointment that followed. What gives his work its edge and its effectiveness is the very directness between the promise and the need, and it is in this respect that his Christian upbringing was so crucial. There were always many types of organised Christianity on offer but it is interesting that only some of them are taken up in the memory of the culture. Internationally the adolescence of Catholic boys has almost become a stock lite-rary situation whereas as far as Protestant England is concerned the emphasis has been almost entirely on the Anglican aesthetic so nurtured in public schools or the collective hymn-singing that contributed to working-class solidarity. Potter stands well aside from these traditions for he is the one product of Gospel Hall fundamentalism who has managed to claim the attention of the nation. All over the country, and not least during the years of Depression, men, women and children went regularly to small halls, many belonging to new evangelical and pentecostal sects in search of a faith that would change their lives and which would be based on a bedrock of certainty. The hallmark of that faith was the emphasis on a personal experience of Christ but what made that experience a possibility and so attractive was that the language of worship was so real and coincided directly with real anxieties, fears and needs. Christ only became real because knowledge of sin was real, salvation was devoutly to be wished because damnation loomed. Grace and atonement were altogether lovely concepts because life itself had been so messy. Very often real faith grew out of an all too real sense of weakness and dread. Of other English writers only Jeanette Winterson has dealt directly with this religious sub-culture and she has shown how her own sense of the absurd and her own developing passion for life distanced her from the certainties of the evangelists. Potter, too, was to be alienated from their crude authoritarianism and from the way in which their power exploited the weaknesses of those in their congregation or family even as it was fuelled by and disguised their own shortcomings. And yet for all his development and success his fundamental needs remained. He could reject the false promises and propaganda and yet still believe that 'all had sinned' and that there would indeed be 'a balm in Gilead'.

Quite central to the evangelical tradition was the realisation that a personal experience of salvation could only occur when a person's real inner voice had openly declared both an awareness of having sinned and the need for a wholeness to be restored. What was essential was that the creeds and formulas of other denominations had to be put aside; here could be no hiding place, no glib recitation. Both in private prayer and in open testimony there had to be a full exposure of the self with the kind of honesty that transcended even that allowed in one's most intimate relationships. In recent years Dennis Potter has developed one of the most distinctive radio voices in the land, and his impact owes much to the fact that he speaks from within that tradition. Quite simply and directly he has made it clear that his illness and his writing are very closely related and that 'the impulse to write' is not a tending of the wound but is the wound itself. Further he admits that 'the need to write is a form of prayer' — prayer, that is, not in the sense of a well-rehearsed liturgy or even as recognition of a great all-forgiving authority and arbiter, but prayer rather as a totally frank admission of all one's own thoughts in which all guilt, all anxiety, all irritation and all anger are released in as blunt a way as possible. The integrity and authenticity of the prayer will be determined only by the degree of honesty and exposure. One does not go to God with an idealised or manicured view of oneself but rather with a full confession of one's inadequacy, sense of evil and need for release. The compulsion comes from within and the acceptance of that is more important than whether there is any response. Even if one's prayer is merely complaint one has fulfilled and recognised a need and established a basis for understanding it.

It is the predisposition towards prayer and testimony that has prompted Dennis Potter to write and which has always made him such an uneasy writer for much of his audience. He has been championed throughout his career by the liberal and radical chattering classes because they assume that his pioneering themes and innovatory techniques were celebrating both their liberation and then their nostalgia. All the while they closed their eyes to his warnings that sin, guilt and violence had not been left behind in the cottages and terraced rows of their childhood. He could never expect much enthusiasm from the conventional middle-classes, from those who believed in total self control and in the suppression of all evil and unseemingly thoughts. He was breaking their every rule and wallowing in what appeared to be self-pity. In general there was little appreciation that his plays were all taking place in the mind, that they were not autobiography or social history but rather investigations of the full implications of certain weaknesses and needs right through to whatever solution, violent or otherwise, was required. The honesty was the thing, as of course was the salvation that came in the resolution. Whatever the fate of the characters, the author's prayer was said and that strand of thought had been articulated and understood. We are invited to share his process of thought and also to celebrate with him both the psychological and artistic triumph. It has been said of Potter that 'he believes in evil', but he also has 'a strong belief in the ability of human beings ultimately to triumph, be loving and conquer the evil in themselves'. This was the judgement, significantly enough, of Jon Amiel, the director of *The Singing Detective*, Potter's most successful, personal and positive play.

It will be as a playwright that Potter will want to be remembered, not as a theologian or psychiatrist, and in this sense it is difficult to relate him to anybody else in British theatre and television. As a dramatist of human weakness and as an exorcist of what must be thought and then controlled he seems to belong far more in the tradition of the modern American stage. O'Neill and Tennessee Williams had paved the way in showing that love, hate, cruelty, sin and redemption could all be found in single families and needed to be articulated and resolved within that immediate context. They had shown, too, something that the English would need to become used too, that one need not be ashamed of preoc- cupations or suspicious of symbols but what was important was the confrontation of what was evil either in thought or deed. There is much that is American in Potter's awareness of how evil and guilt stand distinct from the cultural context, that those things cannot just be suppressed or disguised by the conventions and routines of the family, the community or whatever self-congratu- latory élite fashion has thrown up. Cultures and sub-cultures specialise in selected memories, collective amnesia and duplicity. We may rail against that and yet ultimately, Potter argues, our responsibility is to cure and understand ourselves so that we may become reliable and worthwhile members of that larger group.

He is quite spectacularly and often irritatingly different from anyone else and certainly he continually challenges and subverts a nation and a culture that still more than anything wants to pride itself on its self-restraint, decorum and understatement. All the while the sheer professionalism of his writing attracts an audience that knows that it will be entertained not least by being introduced to so many recognisable aspects of the English experience. All too often there is a subsequent embarrassment as lovely forests and villages and familiar London locations are sullied by dark thoughts and deeds. Why, people ask, has this man unloaded his own disgust on our green and pleasant land? Is that what it's all about? Is that all there is to it — that there were dirty deeds in those lovely woods and behind those cottage doors and that the new world of wine bars and plush suburbs is just as bad? Or is it rather (and surely this is what the plays suggest) that a double process of cleansing is required? Both the evil that is in others and which is so often hypocritically disguised and the evil in oneself must be overcome so that the good things can be enjoyed without reservation and inhibition. And chief amongst those things to be enjoyed is England itself.

He stands in such sharp contrast to so many of our cultural assumptions and yet he remains so very much an English writer. To read the whole of his work is to realise how much he cares about his country, and one aspect of his re-emergence as a public figure in recent years is the glimpse we are given of his obvious enjoyment of so many aspects of English life. He has often said that he only really knows the Forest of Dean and London, those two very self-enclosed worlds at either end of the A40 and the GWR line. He can have no illusions about either; he knows full well of the cruelty and exploitation that both contain. He has been let down and wounded by both places and he has had difficulty in reconciling them: so much of that is in his work. Throughout his adult life he has battled with illness and has disciplined himself into being a prolific and successful writer. We have it on his own word that those two things were always closely related and they certainly loomed as the two great aspects of an immediate reality. He has said less of the things beyond but one always senses their presence — a wife, a family, a home, a London that craves talent, wit and professionalism and is prepared to reward them, the capital city of a great and unique culture and language. And all the while there is that lovely English countryside which he never really left. Is there anywhere lovelier in the world? Of course it's not as innocent or as lovely as it looks. But it could be? Perhaps we can make it so?

References

The Drama of the A40

10 — Hide and Seek (HAS), p.43

10 — The Glittering Coffin (TGC), p.39

12 — Waiting for the Boat (WFTB), p.39

12 — HAS, p.61

12 — WFTB, p.30

12 — HAS, p.40

12 — WFTB, p.22

13 — *ibid.*, p.20

13 —Alex Ward, 'TV's Tormented Master', *New York Times Magazine*, 13 November 1988

13 —WFTB, p.34

14 —HAS, p.41

14 — Norman Mailer, *The Armies of the Night*, Penguin, 1968

15 —Philip Roth, *The Ghost Writer*, Penguin, 1980, p.75

15 — Philip Roth, *The Facts*, 1989, p.3. See also *Patrimony*, Vintage, 1992

16 — *Stand Up, Nigel Barton* (NB), 1965

Does Class Matter?

17 — TGC, p.71

18 — Arthur Marwick, *Culture in Britain Since 1945*, Blackwell,1991

20 — TGC, p.95

20 — *ibid*, p.17

20 — WFTB, p.22

22 — TGC, p.72

22 — *ibid*, p.36

22 — *The Changing Forest* (TCF), p.139

22 — TGC, p.62

23 — *ibid*, p.41

23 — *ibid*, p.77

24 — *ibid*, p.76

24 — Humphrey Phelps, *The Forest of Dean*, Alan Sutton, Gloucester, 1982, p.7

24 — *The Times*, 28 September 1992
25 — Laurie Lee, *Cider with Rosie*, Penguin, 1962, p.184
25 — TCF, p.19
26 — *ibid*, p.46
26 — Phelps, p.23
26 — TCF, p.19
28 — TGC, p.79
28 — *ibid*, p.62
28 — *ibid*, p.12
28 — *ibid*, p.76
28 — TCF, p.21
29 — *ibid*, p.28
29 — *ibid*, p.31
29 — TCF, p.46
29 — *ibid*, p.40
31 — TGC, p.16
31 — Richard Wollheim, 'How It Strikes a Compatriot', *Partisan Review*, no.27, 1960, p.354
31 — TGC, p.13
32 — TCF, p.90
33 — TGC, p.145
33 — *ibid*, Postscript p.ii, and p.28
33 — TGC, p.37
33 — *ibid*, p.51
34 — TGC, p.31
34 — TCF, p.102
34 — TGC, p.40. Potter is discussing Raymond Williams, *The Uses of Literacy*
35 — *ibid*, p.85
36 — Alan Sinfield, *Literature, Culture and Politics in Postwar Britain*, Blackwell, 1989, p.241 *et seq*
38 — TGC, p.122
38 — TCF, p.138
38 — *ibid*, p.94
40 — TCF, p.140
42 — *The Observer*, 2 November 1980, reprinted in Clive James, Glued to the Box, Picador, 1983
43 — Robert Brown, 'Dollars from Hollywood', BFI *Monthly Film Bulletin*, vol.49, no.582, July 1982

A Life in Television

44 — Philip Purser, 'Dennis Potter' in George W. Brandt, *British Television Drama*, Cambridge, 1981, p.168
44 — Philip Purser, *Done Viewing*, Quartet, 1992
44 — Richard Last, 'Bye to the Box', *Daily Telegraph*, 24 July 1992
44 — Philip Purser, 'Do Not Adjust Your Set', *Sunday Telegraph*, 12 July 1992
45 — *ibid*, and *Done Viewing*
46 — Alex Ward, *op cit* p.88
46 — *Daily Mail*, 27 January 1979
46 — *TV Times*, 1 October 1980
47 — WFTB, p.27
47 — e.g. Graeme Turner, *British Cultural Studies: An Introduction*, Unwin Hyman, Boston, 1990
48 — John Tulloch, *Television Drama*, Routledge, 1990
49 — WFTB, p.15, and Brandt, p.1
49 — Brandt, p.173
50 — WFBT, p.12
59 — T.C. Worsley, 'Television, the Ephemeral Art', 1970 (reprinted from *Financial Times*)
59 — New Statesman, 17 December 1965
59 — Sinfield, p.270
70 — Worsley, p.73
71 — Alex Ward, *op cit*, p.86
71 — Hilary Jones and Geoff Tiballs, *Box of Delights*, Macmillan, 1989
71 — *ibid*, p.125
72 — Adam Mars-Jones, 'The Art of Illness', *Independent*, 14 November 1986

Potterland

74 — WFTB, p.17
74 — *ibid*, p.30
75 — ibid, p.19
75 — Mars-Jones, *op cit*
75 — 'Redemption From Under the Skin', *Observer*, 7 December 1986

77 — Dennis Potter, *Son of Man, A Play*, Samuel French, 1970
78 — *ibid*, p.39
79 — WFTB, p.20 and p.89
79 — *Joe's Ark*, text in WFTB, p.112
79 — Brandt, p.188
83 — Kingsley and Tibballs, p.125
84 — Brandt, p.180 *et seq*
84 — Kingsley and Tibballs, p.112
86 — HAS, p.27
86 — *ibid*, p.37
87 — ibid, p.82
88 —see cover of Dennis Potter, *Brimstone and Treacle, A Play*, Samuel French, 1978
90 — ibid
91 — *New York Times*, 10 July 1989, p.C16
91 — Brandt, p.187
97 — John Wyver, 'Paradise Perhaps', *Time Out*, 9 March 1978
97 — Patrick Wright, *Guardian*, 15 February 1993
99 — *The Independent Magazine*, 17 March 1990
99 — Ira D. Sankey, *Sacred Songs and Solos*, Butler & Tanner, Frome, Hymn 237
101 — BFI *Monthly Film Bulletin*, vol.49, no.582, July 1982, p.127
102 — Robert Brown, *ibid*

Potter At Large

105 — 'The Tortured Playwright Who Went Wrong', *Sunday Telegraph* Profile, 31 December 1989
106 — WFTB, p.40. The text of *Blue Remembered Hills* (ibid) ends with the Housman two verse poem 'Into my heart an air that kills' from *A Shropshire Lad*. In the broadcast it is Potter's voice that we hear reciting the poem.
112 — Patrick Wright, *op cit*
112 — David Gritten, 'Come Back Mr Potter', *Telegraph Magazine*, 2 January 1993
112 — Record sleeve, *The Singing Detective*, BBC Records, EMI, 1986
116 — Dennis Potter, *Sufficient Carbohydrate*, Faber, 1983, p.55

122 — See Richard Grant on Potter and the BBC, *Evening News*, 21 May 1979; 'Why British TV is Going to the Dogs', *Daily Mail*, 30 July 1980; Patrick Stoddart, *Sunday Times*, 26 November 1989

123 — HAS, p.115

124 — WFTB, p.33

124 — *Sunday Telegraph*, 31 December 1989, and Ginny Dougary, *Times Saturday Review*, 26 September 1992, p.8

124 — For Trodd see Patrick Stoddart, *Sunday Times*, 26 November 1989; Brian Robertson was reviewing *Blackeyes* on BBC Radio 3's *The Critics*, 2 December 1989

128 —Stephen Holden, 'Their Songs Were America's Happy Talk', *New York Times*, 24 January 1992

129 — *Sunday Telegraph*, 31 December 1989

129 — *Independent Magazine*, 17 March 1990

130 — Jeanette Winterson's novel *Oranges Are Not The Only Fruit* was first published by Pandora in 1985 and dramatized by BBC TV in 1991. See also Megan Tressider, 'Profiting from the Wilderness', *Sunday Telegraph*, 6 September 1992

130 — In conversation with Rosemary Harthill, BBC Radio 4, 27 December 1991

132 — *Sunday Times*, 23 November 1986

Bibliography

Listed here are the works of Dennis Potter referrred to in this volume. For fuller details see Philip Purser on 'Dennis Potter' in George W. Brandt, *British Television Drama*, CUP, 1991, and Graham Fuller (ed), *Potter on Potter*, Faber and Faber, 1993.

Television Plays

The Confidence Course, 1965, BBC1
Alice, 1965, BBC1
Stand Up, Nigel Barton, 1965, BBC1
Vote, Vote, Vote for Nigel Barton, 1965, BBC1
Where the Buffalo Roam, 1966, BBC1
Message for Posterity, 1967, BBC1
A Beast With Two Backs, 1968, BBC1
Moonlight On The Highway, 1969, LWT/Kestrel
Son of Man, 1969, BBC1
Lay Down Your Arms, 1970, LWT/Kestrel
Angels Are So Few, 1970, BBC1
Traitor, 1971, BBC1
Casanova (6 parts), 1971, BBC2
Follow the Yellow Brick Road, 1972, BBC2
Only Make Believe, 1973, BBC1
Joe's Ark, 1974, BBC1
Schmoedipus, 1974, BBC1
Late Call (4 parts), 1975, BBC2
Double Dose, 1976, BBC2
Brimstone and Treacle, 1976, BBC1 (first shown in 1987)
Where Adam Stood, 1976, BBC2
Pennies From Heaven (6 parts), 1978, BBC1
Blue Remembered Hills, 1979, BBC1
The Singing Detective (6 parts), 1986, BBC1
Blackeyes (6 parts), 1989, BBC/ABC/TN2
Lipstick On Your Collar (6 parts), 1993, Channel 4

Feature Films

Pennies from Heaven (1981) USA
Brimstone and Treacle (1982) UK
Dreamchild (1985) UK
Track 29 (1987) UK (shot in USA)
Secret Friends (1992) UK

Books

Non-Fiction

The Glittering Coffin, Gollancz, 1960
The Changing Forest, Secker & Warburg, 1962

Fiction

Hide and Seek, Andre Deutsch, 1973, Faber and Faber, 1990
Pennies From Heaven, Quartet Books, 1981
Ticket to Ride, Faber and Faber, 1986
Blackeyes, Faber and Faber, 1987

Published Plays

The Nigel Barton Plays, Penguin, 1967
Son of Man, Samuel French, 1970
Follow the Yellow Brick Road (in Robert Muller, ed., *The Television Dramatist*, Elek, 1973)
Brimstone and Treacle, Samuel French, 1978
Sufficient Carbohydrate, Faber and Faber, 1983
Waiting For the Boat, On Television, Faber and Faber, 1984 (includes *Blue Remembered Hills, Joe's Ark* and *Cream in my Coffee)*
The Singing Detetctive, Faber & Faber, 1986
Lipstick On Your Collar, Faber and Faber, 1993

Selected Bibliography

Philip Barnes, *A Companion to Post-War British Theatre*, Barnes and Noble, 1986

Tony Bennett (ed), *Popular Television and Film*, BFI, 1981

D.J. Enright, *Fields of Vision: Essays on Literature, Language and Television*, OUP, 1988

Boris Ford (ed), *Modern Britain*, The Cambridge Cultural History of Britain, vol.9, CUP, 1992

Richard Hoggart, *The Uses of Literacy*, Chatto and Windus, 1957

Robert Hewison, *In Anger: Culture in the Cold War*, Weidenfeld, 1981

Robert Hewison, *Too Much: Art and Modern Society in the Sixties*, Methuen, 1986

Brian Jackson & Dennis Marsden, *Education and the Working Class*, Routledge, 1982

Clive James, *Glued to the Box*, Picador, 1983

Clive James, *On Television*, Picador, 1991

Hilary Kingsley & Geoff Tibballs, *Box of Delights: The Golden Years of Television*, Macmillan, 1989

Stuart Laing, *Representations of Working Class Life 1957-1964*, Macmillan, 1986

Arthur Marwick, *Culture in Britain Since 1945*, Blackwell, 1991

Tom Maschler, *Declaration*, MacGibbon & Kee, 1957

Tony Palmer, *All You Need Is Love*, Futura, 1977

Humphrey Phelps, *The Forest of Dean*, Alan Sutton, 1982

Philip Purser, *Done Viewing*, Quartet, 1992

Alan Sinfield, *Literature, Politics and Culture in Postwar Britain*, Blackwell, 1989

John Tulloch, *Television, Drama, Agency, Audience and Myth*, Routledge, 1990

Graeme Turner, *British Cultural Studies: An Introduction*, Unwin Hyman, 1990

Raymond Williams, *Culture and Society 1780-1950*, Chatto & Windus, 1958

Raymond Williams, *The Long Revolution*, Chatto & Windus, 1961

Raymond Williams, *Television, Technology and Cultural Form*, Fontana, 1974

T.C. Worsley, *Television, the Ephemeral Art*, Alan Ross, 1970

Selected Profiles, Interviews and Analysis

Robert Brown, 'Dollars from Hollywood', BFI *Monthly Film Bulletin*, vol.49, no.582, July 1992

E. Jane Dickson, 'Potter Back On Song', *Radio Times*, 20 February 1993

Ginny Dougary, 'Potter's Weal', *Times Saturday Review*, 26 September 1992

Graham Fuller, *Potter on Potter*, Faber and Faber, 1993

David Gritten, 'Come Back Mr Potter', *Telegraph Magazine*, 2 January 1993

Paul Johnson, 'The Potter Calls the Digger Black', *Spectator*, 3 April 1993

Mark Lawson, 'Skin Flicks', *Independent Magazine*, 13 February 1993

Adam Mars-Jones, 'The Art of Illness', *Independent*, 14 November 1986

David Nathan, 'Private Pottah's Post-War Work' *Sunday Telegraph*, 14 February 1993

Observer Profile, 'Redemption from Under the Skin', *Observer*, 7 December 1986

John J. O'Connor, 'An Unlikely Hero Copes', *New York Times*, 10 July 1989

Philip Purser, 'Dennis Potter' in George W. Brandt, *British Television Drama*, CUP, 1981

Philip Purser, 'Deep, Dark and Dangerous', *Telegraph TV and Radio*, 20 February 1993

Philip Purser, 'Do Not Adjust Your Set', *Sunday Telegraph*, 12 July 1992

Sunday Telegraph Profile, 'The Tortured Playwright Who Went Wrong', *Sunday Telegraph*, 31 November 1989

Patrick Stoddart, 'Teetering on the Edge of Darkness', *Sunday Times*, 26 November 1989

Christopher Tookey, 'Dennis Potter's Dark Vision', *Sunday Telegraph*, 3 December 1989

BIBLIOGRAPHY

Sally Vincent, 'The Elusive Dennis Potter', *Cosmopolitan*, December 1987

Alex Ward, 'TV's Tormented Master', *New York Times Magazine*, 13 November 1988

Richard Wollheim, 'How It Strikes a Compatriot', *Partisan Review*, no.27, 1960

Patrick Wright, 'The Last Acre of Truth', *Guardian*, 15 February 1993

John Wyver, 'Paradise Perhaps', *Time Out*, 9 March 1978

Series Afterword

The Border country is that region between England and Wales which is upland and lowland, both and neither. Centuries ago kings and barons fought over these Marches without their national allegiance ever being settled. In our own time, referring to his childhood, that eminent borderman Raymond Williams once said: 'We talked of "The English" who were not us, and "The Welsh" who were not us.' It is beautiful, gentle, intriguing, and often surprising. It displays majestic landscapes, which show a lot, and hide some more. People now walk it, poke into its cathedrals and bookshops, and fly over or hang-glide from its mountains, yet its mystery remains.

In cultural terms the region is as fertile as (in parts) its agriculture and soil. The continued success of the Three Choirs Festival and the growth of the border town of Hay as a centre of the secondhand book trade have both attracted international recognition. The present series of introductory books is offered in the light of such events. Writers as diverse as Mary Webb, Raymond Williams and Wilfred Owen are seen in the special light — perhaps that cloudy, golden twilight so characteristic of the region — of their origin in this area or association with it. There are titles too, though fewer, on musicians and painters. The Gloucestershire composers such as Samuel Sebastian Wesley, and painters like David Jones, bear an imprint of border woods, rivers, villages and hills.

How wide is the border? Two, five or fifteen miles each side of the boundary; it depends on your perspective, on the placing of the nearest towns, on the terrain itself, and on history. In the time of Offa and after, Hereford itself was a frontier town, and Welsh was spoken there even in the nineteenth century. True border folk traditionally did not recognize those from even a few miles away. Today, with greater mobility, the crossing of boundaries is easier, whether for education, marriage, art or leisure. For myself, who spent some childhood years in Herefordshire and a decade of middle-age crossing between England and Wales once a week, I can only say that as you approach the border you feel it. Suddenly you are in that finally elusive terrain, looking from a bare height down on to the plain, or from the lower land up to a gap in the hills, and you want to explore it, maybe not to return.

This elusiveness pertains to the writers and artists too. It is often difficult to decide who is border, to what extent and with what impact on their work. The urbane Elizabeth Barrett Browning, prominent figure of the salons of London and Italy in her time, spent virtually all her life until her late twenties outside Ledbury in Herefordshire, and this fact is being seen by current critics and scholars as of more and more significance. The twentieth century 'English pastoral' composers — with names like Parry, Howells, and Vaughan Williams — were nearly all border people. One wonders whether border country is now suddenly found on the English side of the Severn Bridge, and how far even John Milton's *Comus*, famous for its first production in Ludlow Castle, is in any sense such a work. Then there is the fascinating Uxbridge-born Peggy Eileen Whistler, transposed in the 1930s into Margiad Evans to write her (epilepsis-based) visionary novels set near her adored Ross-on-Wye and which today still retain a magical charm. Further north: could Barbara Pym, born and raised in Oswestry, even remotely be called a border writer? Most people would say that the poet A.E. Housman was far more so, yet he hardly ever visited the county after which his chief book of poems, *A Shropshire Lad*, is named. Further north still: there is the village of Chirk on the boundary itself, where R.S. Thomas had his first curacy; there is Gladstone's Hawarden Library, just outside Chester and actually into Clwyd in Wales itself; there is intriguingly the Wirral town of Birkenhead, where Wilfred Owen spent his adolescence and where his fellow war poet the Welsh Eisteddfod winner Hedd Wynn was awarded his Chair — posthumously.

On the Welsh side the names are different. The mystic Ann Griffiths; the metaphysical poet Henry Vaughan; the astonishing nineteenth century symbolist novelist Arthur Machen (in Linda Dowling's phrase, 'Pater's prose as registered by Wilde'); and the remarkable Thomas Olivers of Gregynog, associated with the writing of the well-known hymn 'Lo He comes with clouds descending'. Those descending clouds...; in border country the scene hangs overhead, and it is easy to indulge in unwarranted speculation. Most significant perhaps is the difference to the two peoples on either side. From England, the border meant the enticement of emptiness, a strange unpopulated land, going up and up into the hills. From Wales, the border meant the road to London, to the university, or to employment, whether by droving sheep, or later to the industries of Birmingham and Liverpool. It also meant the enemy, since borders and boundaries are necessarily political. Much is shared, yet different languages are spoken, in more than one sense.

With certain notable exceptions, the books in this series are short introductory studies of one person's work or some aspect of it. There are no indexes. The bibliography lists main sources referred to in the text, and sometimes others, for anyone who would like to pursue the topic further. The authors reflect the diversity of their subjects. They are specialists or academics; critics or biographers; poets or musicans themselves; or ordinary people with, however, an established reputation of writing imaginatively and directly about what moves them. They are of various ages, both sexes, Welsh and English, border people themselves or from further afield.

To those who explore the matter, the subjects — the writers, painters and composers written about — seem increasingly to be united by a particular kind of vision. This holds good however diverse they are in other, main ways; and of course they are diverse indeed. One might scarcely associate, it would seem, Raymond Williams with Samuel Sebastian Wesley, or Dennis Potter with Thomas Traherne. But one has to be careful in such assumptions. The epigraph to Bruce Chatwin's twentieth century novel *On the Black Hill* is a passage from the seventeenth century mystic writer Jeremy Taylor. Thomas Traherne himself is the subject of a recent American study which puts Traherne's writings into dialogue with the European philosopher-critics Martin Heidegger, Jacques Derrida and Jacques Lacan. And a current bestselling writer of thrillers, Ellis Peters, sets her stories in a Shrewsbury of the late medieval Church with a cunning quiet monk as her ever-engaging sleuth.

The vision (name incidentally of the farmhouse in Chatwin's novel) is something to do with the curious border light already mentioned. To avoid getting sentimental and mystic here — though border writers have at times been both — one might suggest literally that this effect is meteorological. Maybe the sun's rays are refracted through skeins of dew or mist that hit the stark mountains and low hills at curious ascertainable angles, with prismatic results. Not that rainbows are the point in our area: it is more the contrasts of gold, green and grey. Some writers never mention it. They don't have to. But all the artists of the region see it, are affected by it, and transpose their highly different emanations of reality through its transparencies. Meanwhile, on the ground, the tourist attractions draw squads from diverse cultural and ethnic origins; agriculture enters the genetic-engineering age; New Age travellers are welcome and unwelcome; and the motorway runs up parallel past all — 'Lord of the M5', as the poet Geoffrey Hill has dubbed the Saxon king Offa, he of the dyke which bisects the region where it can still be identified. The region has its uniqueness, then, and a statistically above-average number of writers and artists (we have identified over fifty clear candidates so far) have drawn something from it, which it is the business of this present series to elucidate.

Peter Stead's riveting interview of Dennis Potter was one of the highlights of the 1993 Hay-on-Wye Festival of Literature: few who were there are likely to forget it. Potter's ability to make the romantic Forest of Dean seem both the whole world and the murky setting of unmentionable scenes from youth and childhood has made him television drama's international leader. The vulnerable characters, painful memories, music-and-sex fantasy, in a landscape connoting everything that "green" has ever meant, is the subject of the present study. Peter Stead seems to enter the medium, the very element period by period, in which Potter moved. It is a necessary commitment in any overview of Dennis Potter's work.

John Powell Ward

The Author

Peter Stead was born in Barry in 1943. He was educated at Barry and Gowerton Grammar Schools and at University College, Swansea, where he is now a Senior Lecturer in History. He has twice been a Visiting Fulbright Scholar in the USA, at Wellesley College, Massachusetts, in 1973-4 and at the University of North Carolina at Wilmington in 1988-9. He is the author of *Coleg Harlech* (1976), *Film and the Working Class* (1989, 1991) and *Richard Burton: So Much, So Little* (1991). For BBC Wales he wrote and presented a television film on *How Green Was My Valley* (1991) and he is a frequent radio broadcaster.

Also in this series

Bruce Chatwin
Eric Gill & David Jones at Capel-y-Ffin
A.E. Housman
Francis Kilvert
Wilfred Owen
Philip Wilson Steer
Mary Webb
Samuel Sebastian Wesley
Raymond Williams